Isle of \

Jackie and Chris Parry

experience   explore   enjoy

FOXGLOVE VISITOR GUIDES

For Jonathan

Published in the UK by
Foxglove Publishing Ltd
Foxglove House
Shute Hill
Lichfield WS13 8DB
England
Tel 01543 673594
1st Edition 2012
ISBN 978 0 95645 606 9

Printed by Gomer Press, Llandysul
Artwork and design by Nicholas Leach

Front cover: Freshwater Bay.
Page 1: Freshwater Bay.
Picture credits: all photos by Andrew Cooke, except Isle of Wight Tourism – www.islandbreaks.co.uk 3 (last but one), 9 (top), 10, 12, 13, 15, 17 (main), 19 (top), 25 (top), 34, 36, 41 (main), 49, 51 (bottom), 59 (both), 75 (both), 77, 80, 85 (inset); authors 6 (Postcard Museum, Roman Villa), 73, 81 (bottom), 84; English Heritage 6 (Osborne Ho), 46, 47; Nicholas Leach 16, 28, 41 (inset), 61. Cartography by Jonathan Young.

JACKIE PARRY has enjoyed an extensive career in tourism and served as President of the Institute of Tourist Guiding. Fluent in French and German, she works as a Blue Badge Guide, taking British and foreign visitors around Southern England, specialising in the Isle of Wight.

CHRIS PARRY is a consultant, writer and academic lecturer on strategic and military themes, who also takes time to enjoy historical studies and a range of outdoor activities.

PHOTOGRAPHS The majority of the photographs in this guide were taken by Andrew Cooke, a keen landscape and maritime photographer. Born and raised in Freshwater, Andrew works as a clock repairer and, along with his wife Donna, devotes his spare time to photographing scenery and events across the Island as well as maritime activity throughout the Solent region.

THIS GUIDE The authors have neither requested nor received payment for the inclusion of any of the amenities or businesses named or recommended in this guide. It has been our intention to present an objective, balanced view of what is available on the Isle of Wight for the benefit of all visitors.

DISCLAIMER While every care has been taken to ensure that the information in this book is as accurate as possible at publication, the publishers and authors accept no responsibility for any loss, injury or inconvenience sustained by anyone using this book. Opening times should be checked before making a visit.

Contents

Isle of Wight

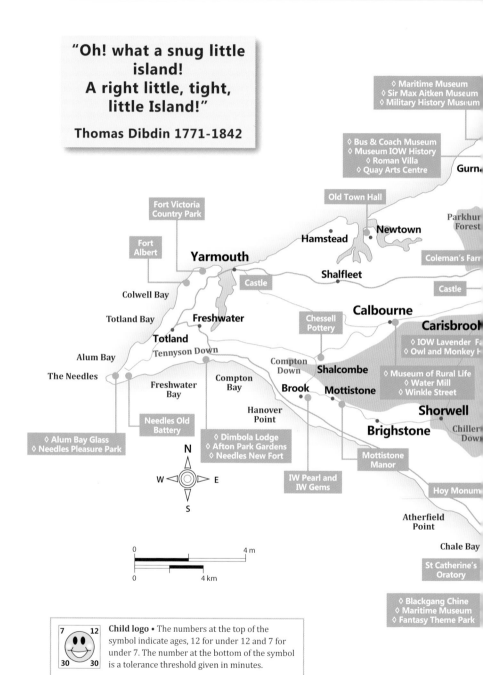

"Oh! what a snug little island!
A right little, tight, little Island!"

Thomas Dibdin 1771-1842

◊ Maritime Museum
◊ Sir Max Aitken Museum
◊ Military History Museum

◊ Bus & Coach Museum
◊ Museum IOW History
◊ Roman Villa
◊ Quay Arts Centre

Gurn

Old Town Hall

Parkhur
Forest

Newtown

Hamstead

Fort Victoria
Country Park

Fort
Albert

Yarmouth

Shalfleet

Coleman's Far

Castle

Colwell Bay

Castle

Calbourne

Totland Bay

Freshwater

Chessell
Pottery

Carisbrook

Totland

Tennyson Down

◊ IOW Lavender F
◊ Owl and Monkey H

Alum Bay

Compton
Down

Shalcombe

◊ Museum of Rural Life
◊ Water Mill
◊ Winkle Street

The Needles

Compton
Bay

Brook

Mottistone

Freshwater
Bay

Shorwell

Hanover
Point

Needles Old
Battery

Brighstone

Chiller
Dow

◊ Alum Bay Glass
◊ Needles Pleasure Park

N

◊ Dimbola Lodge
◊ Afton Park Gardens
◊ Needles New Fort

Mottistone
Manor

W   E

IW Pearl and
IW Gems

Hoy Monum

S

Atherfield
Point

0   4 m

Chale Bay

0   4 km

St Catherine's
Oratory

◊ Blackgang Chine
◊ Maritime Museum
◊ Fantasy Theme Park

Child logo • The numbers at the top of the symbol indicate ages, 12 for under 12 and 7 for under 7. The number at the bottom of the symbol is a tolerance threshold given in minutes.

4

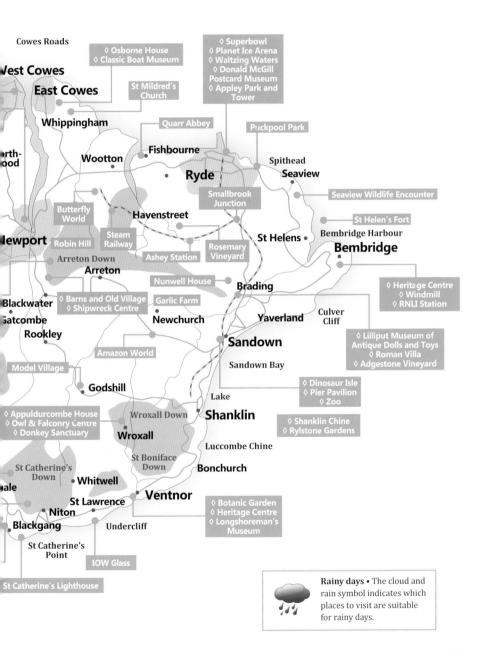

Rainy days • The cloud and rain symbol indicates which places to visit are suitable for rainy days.

TopTips

Here is the authors' personal choice of their favourite attractions that should give most visitors an appreciation of what the Isle of Wight has to offer.

Osborne House
Victoria's Retreat

Carisbrooke Castle
Bite-size history

Isle of Wight Steam Railway
Nostalgia rules

Amazon World
Sub-tropical surprise

Tennyson Trail
Great views

Ventnor Botanic Gardens
Visually impressive

Donald McGill Postcard Museum
Saucy Ryde

Brading Roman Villa
Mosaics and more

Dimbola Lodge
Cameras, cakes and coffee

Quarr Abbey
Quiet, but evocative

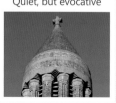

Dinosaur Isle
Hands-on bones experience

Newtown Estuary
Coastal Nature Reserve

Welcome

Climate • When To Go • Geography •
Double Tide • Geology • Brief
History • Wildlife • Flora and Fauna •
Wildflowers • Character

Welcome to the Isle of Wight

Why should anyone want to go to the Isle of Wight? In the first place, travelling to any island by sea has a hint of excitement and the exotic about it; the crossing not only places the traveller in a normally unfamiliar sea environment, but also induces a definite break in thinking and routine. The passage to the Isle of Wight has all the thrill of going abroad, but without the loss of those familiar features which make the United Kingdom home.

Some people have travelled to the Island in the past as eccentrics, recluses or fugitives or in search of inspiration. A great many come because of an intuitive need to return to a place where they remember spending happy childhood holidays. Many retire to the Island, while others seek a commercial opportunity. Both scenically and culturally, the Isle of Wight is a miniature replica of the south-east of England. It has a balanced diversity of town and country landscapes, of brashness and sophistication, of modernity and tradition, providing for a broad spectrum of tastes. It has a varied, stimulating historical and literary heritage, with enough monuments, curiosities and memorials to satisfy the most enthusiastic professional tourist or incurable romantic.

Furthermore, it is suitable for both long and short trips and the Island's diverse yet self-contained appeal often induces visitors to return. Finally, there is the mild climate and sea air, which has been known, particularly since early Victorian times, for its restorative and inspirational powers. Whatever the attraction or reason, visitors have always come in their thousands and continue to do so, despite the magnetic pull of holidays abroad. J. B. Priestley probably summed it up best when he said that one, 'might take one glance at the Island as something on a map, and then decide to give it a couple of hours. But you can spend days and days exploring the Isle of Wight, which, if you are really interested, begins magically enlarging itself for you.'

Climate

The climate is affected mainly by the prevalence of sea breezes and by the high incidence of south-westerly winds. Topography also plays a part, which is why the coast between Blackgang and Luccombe is so mild, protected from all but southerly winds and exposed to the sunny south. Conversely, Ventnor in summer is slightly cooler owing to its cliff-top position in relative shade at the start and end of the day and the cool south-westerlies which prevail at that time of year. Throughout the year, the Island is one to two degrees higher in temperature than the mainland.

When To Go

There is something to do on the Island all the year round, despite the seasonal emphasis of some businesses and attractions. The variety of attractions in a small area and the transport infrastructure mean that the vagaries of the weather can be mitigated at any time. However, opening times of most attractions are curtailed in the winter months and some, more obviously 'tourist orientated', close

▼ Wightlink ferry takes you to the Island.

down altogether. The larger, less seasonally dependent attractions and those in the towns generally stay open during winter daylight hours. It is worth checking before planning a visit out of season.

The periods from Easter to early summer and September to the end of October offer the best balance of weather and amenities, when the popular resorts and attractions are not too crowded. From June through to August anyone wanting sun and a beach-centred holiday is likely to be most content. These periods are the most suitable for longer trips of one or two weeks. In winter the weekend break or day trip is likely to prove the most rewarding, although themed trips, based on particular interests may extend a visit. Accommodation is normally cheaper off season, but choice will be more restricted.

Those with special interests, such as bird-watching, will wish to gear their visits to periods of optimum activity. Migrant birds are best observed on one of the main migration routes in spring or autumn. Walkers and cyclists will find suitable routes all year round. Sailing and other water sports are naturally inhibited in winter, although the more experienced, adventurous wind and board surfers and yachties will no doubt find the challenge exhilarating.

Geography

The Isle of Wight is a lozenge shaped island, measuring twenty-three miles (37km) from the Needles in the west to Bembridge Foreland in the east and thirteen miles (21km) from Cowes in the north to St Catherine's Point in the south. It is about sixty miles

▲ Winter walkers enjoying the Island's stunning coastline.

▼ The passenger hovercraft which runs from Ryde to Southsea.

9

▲ Yacht racing at Cowes.

(97km) all round and covers about 155 square miles (401km²), with a population of 140,000. It fits snugly against the opposite mainland of Hampshire and is separated by the narrow stretch of water known as the Solent, which varies in width from six miles (9.7km) to about three quarters of a mile (1km).

Double Tide

An odd Solent phenomenon is its double high tide, which was so distinct as to be mentioned in Bede's 'History of the English Church and People' in the eighth century. The first tide comes straight up the English Channel through the Needles Channel from the west and produces the first high water. Two hours later, another tide, which started out in the Atlantic about twelve hours before the first one, and flogged its way around the top of Scotland and through the Dover Straits, arrives from the east. Just as the (first) tide is starting to ebb, it returns to a high tide again (with the second), before ebbing rapidly to complete the cycle. This has given the Solent distinctive tidal features and considerable problems for the unwary, careless navigator or sporting sailor.

A spine of chalk hills, or downs, running east to west, from Sandown to the Needles, virtually bisects the Island and another outcrop behind St Catherine's and Shanklin hems in the Undercliff, on the south-east side of the lozenge. The main river is the Medina, which almost traverses the Island from south to north, passing through Newport and emptying into the sea at Cowes. Numerous bays, chines and tidal creeks indent the coast.

Geology

Geologically, the Island presents a unique and complex amalgam of layers or strata. Specialist geologists enthuse about the concentration of so many different types of rock and geological periods in one small area, but even the casual but perceptive visitor will note the sudden changes in topography and rock types across the Island. The very old Wealden

Beds near Sandown and the compelling east-west spine of chalk are supplemented elsewhere by clays, gravels and greensands.

Whitecliff Bay is a striking example of where the chalk and clay meet, to be joined by a whole sequence of important sedimentary layers in order of the time they were deposited. Consequently, the Island is well-known for its fossil finds: the Wealden Beds have revealed the fossilised skeletons of large reptiles and the whole coastline of West Wight from Atherfield Ledge through Alum Bay to Hamstead has produced prolific numbers of plant and animal fossils.

Underlying 'Blue Slipper' clay was responsible for the landslip (hence its name) that caused the Undercliff in the south-east of the Island. All in all, it is a geologist's paradise and those who want to delve more deeply should visit Dinosaur Isle in Sandown, Britain's first purpose-built Dinosaur Museum, which houses the Island's fossil and geology collection.

The Isle of Wight's existence as an Island dates from about 8,000 years ago, when the sea breached the continuous chalk ridge between the Needles and the Isle of Purbeck, in mainland Dorset. Before that event, a river had flowed down Southampton Water and emptied into the sea via the channel of the eastern Solent somewhere south of Littlehampton.

Brief History

Archaeological remains have revealed human settlement from the Old Stone Age and implements from at least Palaeolithic times (half a million years to 12,000 years ago). Further evidence of settlement is provided by Neolithic (2,300-1,900BC) long barrows along the Downs and numerous Bronze Age (about 1,900BC onwards) round barrows. Iron Age occupation (from about 550BC), demonstrated by ancient field systems and one hill fort on Chillerton Down, gave way to

▼ On the coast.

Isle of Wight Welcome

▲ The Isle of Wight is Red Squirrel territory.

Roman domination after Claudius' invasion of Britain in 43 AD.

The Island, called *Ynys yr wyth* (the Island of the channel), was captured by the II Legion, commanded by the future emperor Vespasian. To the Romans, the Island was known as 'Vectis' and its agricultural output is attested by the surviving remains of several large villas, including those at Brading and Newport. It was once thought that a fort lay under Carisbrooke Castle, but no Roman town or road has been identified.

In the confused settlement after the Roman era in the fifth century, the Island was initially seized and held by Jutish war-bands, but they, in turn, were replaced by West Saxons. According to Bede, the inhabitants of the Island had remained defiantly pagan up to that point, but from then on had their own bishop, subject to the See of Winchester. The rest of the Anglo-Saxon period was punctuated with raids by Scandinavian or Viking marauders. One most memorably led to a sea battle at Brading won by Alfred the Great's forces in 896.

After the Norman Conquest in 1066, the Island was granted to William I's close friend and senior military commander, William fitzOsbern. He started the building of Carisbrooke castle with a motte-and-bailey structure and endowed its priory and six Island churches. In 1100, the lordship of the Island passed to the de Redvers family who held it until 1293, when Edward I purchased the lordship and took it into Crown hands.

During the late medieval and Tudor period, the Island became progressively more involved and integrated with events and personalities on the mainland. From the fourteenth to the sixteenth century, the Isle of Wight and the coastline opposite were constantly exposed to raids by the French, especially during the 100 Years' War and in the reign of Henry VIII (1509-47). In the Civil Wars of 1642-8, the Island assumed national prominence when Charles I was held at Carisbrooke and tried to escape while negotiating terms with Parliament and the Army.

The Island's subsequent history was shaped by the importance of the Solent as a focus for trade and its association with the rise of the Royal Navy. During the long periods of war in the eighteenth century, the Isle of Wight was notorious for widespread smuggling and excise evasion, while it helped meet the needs of the growing military and commercial effort. Thereafter, the patronage of Queen Victoria at Osborne and the rise of tourism did much to transform the Island into an attractive and popular resort.

Mammals

There are thirty-seven species of mammal on the Island. Hedgehogs and moles are common and there are ten species of bat, while rabbits and hares are evenly distributed throughout. Badgers, foxes, weasels and stoats are frequently seen in country areas, together with the occasional otter, which has swum from the mainland, but rarely stays. The only deer have been introduced on farms as stock.

The Isle of Wight is one of the few places where the red squirrel can be seen. There are about 3,000 red squirrels in the Island's woodlands, particularly in Parkhurst Forest. A naturalist has stated with some irony: 'The grey squirrel occasionally comes over on the ferries, but has not become established here'.

Birds

The Island supports a changing resident and migratory bird population. There are a great many sea and coastal nesting locations, with the main sites at Freshwater and Culver Cliff. Cormorants, shags, wintering grebes, waders, wildfowl (Canada geese) can all be found in northern creeks and around Brading (RSPB Bird Hide). A recent decline in guillemots and razorbills has been accompanied by a rise in peregrines, which have colonised Freshwater, and fulmars, which can be seen from Blackgang to Culver Cliff.

The barn owl is a common sight at dusk, although the tawny owl is not seen on the Island. Other distinctive species are: the green and great spotted woodpeckers, the collared dove and a few pairs of Dartford

warblers. Ravens and rooks, which have recently been under threat, have managed to survive modern changes in their habitats.

For migratory birds, the best time of year is from March to May at St Catherine's Lighthouse where the passage is from east to west and where special perches have been set up. Divers, waders, auks, terns and skuas can be seen, as well as ducks and large numbers of smaller land birds. In autumn, Fort Victoria on the Freshwater Peninsula is the best vantage point for witnessing the reverse migration from east to west.

Reptiles

The grass snake, the adder, slow-worm and common lizard are all to be found on the Island, while frogs, toads and three types of newt are also widely distributed.

Butterflies

The Island is particularly rich in butterflies. The grass of the downland, which has its own distinctive species of plants, is home to a wide variety, including the chalk hill blue and the adonis blue. The small blue can be found in relative abundance around Compton and Afton Downs.

Wight is a good habitat for fritillaries; the dark green and silver-washed are found on the Downs, Parkhurst Forest holds small and brown pearl-bordered and marsh varieties, Newtown and Hamstead the high brown. The Glanville fritillary is unique (in the UK) to the Isle of Wight and is found from late spring along the cliffs in the south-east of the Island.

Today, despite continuing agricultural activity, the Island relies heavily on visitors, leisure activities and residential development to sustain its vitality and economy. Improved transport links with the mainland allow people to settle on the Island and commute to work across the water. Although the Isle of Wight shares some services with nearby Hampshire, since 1974 it has been a separate administrative county. It is geographically the largest parliamentary constituency in the country.

Flora and Fauna

A trip to the Isle of Wight presents an ideal opportunity to introduce visitors and their children to the pleasures of the Island's wildlife. The mild climate and sea air, separation from the mainland, and the different habitats induced by the topography and geology are reflected in the wildlife which can be seen on the Island. Many species found on the mainland opposite, such as the grey squirrel, the nuthatch and the sand lizard, are not found in the Island.

Wild flowers

Two woodland flowers which thrive on the Island are, uniquely, the wood calamint and the more widely known wild columbine. Most woodland supports wild garlic with its distinctive aroma and non-native cord-grass has colonised the edges and mudflats of most of the northern estuaries and creeks. There are also twenty seven species of orchid. Some of them are plentiful, such as the common spotted or the early-purple; others are less common, but can be found on the chalk downs, such as the bee and the pyramidal orchids.

Nature Areas on the Island

A particular favourite is Walter's Copse and Town Copse (National Trust) at Newtown, with their well-established and accessible path systems. Newtown is a delightful silted creek, which has salt marshes, tidal mud flats and shingle banks. There are black-headed gulls in profusion, together with wild fowl, waders and terns. Cord-grass grows in abundance and it is just about the only place on the Island to hear and see the nightingale, which thrives on the blackthorn and damp thickets. Other places suitable for laymen, with car parks or lay-bys, to explore the wildlife are:

- America Wood, Shanklin (Woodland Trust), pictured.
- Borthwood Copse, Alverstone (National Trust).
- Brighstone Forest, mixed woodland walk over about 2.5 miles (4km).
- Combley Great Wood, near Havenstreet.
- Firestone Copse, near Wootton (Forest Enterprise) has waymarked walks.
- Parkhurst Forest (Forest Enterprise), 2.5-mile (4km) walk with shorter trails.
- River Medina, Newport has 300 acres (122 hectares) of saltmarsh, woodland and river, with a two-mile (3.2km) walk, starting at Newport Quay.

There are many dedicated woodland and wildlife trails and walks, which have been set up by the Forest Enterprise and other agencies. Some are mentioned in the text, or can be accessed via www.islandbreaks.co.uk. The Isle of Wight Council's Countryside Section (Tel 01983 823893) also organises an excellent programme of countryside events from April to September, mostly based around walks. There is no need to book, but there may be a nominal charge.

▲ Thatched Island cottages.

Character

Conscious of its pre-Victorian remoteness and its tradition of sturdy self-reliance, the Island is proud of its separation – rather than isolation – from the rest of the United Kingdom. Its people have stoutly resisted all attempts to link it with the mainland by means of a bridge or tunnel. 'Caulkheads', those born on the Island and from established Island families, are still keen to maintain their status against the 'overners', who are not natives by birth and 'grockles', as tourists are known. Denizens of Ryde or Yarmouth still talk about 'going to England' or, wryly, refer to England as the North Island.

Agriculture and market gardening (particularly organic) enterprises are thriving although employing fewer people every year. The Island's industry and manufacturing base is excessively light for a local mixed economy and the Island depends overwhelmingly on attracting visitors.

The Island is having to attract more visitors to sustain its economy while maintaining an

▼ The south coast of the Island from Blackgang to Tennyson Down.

Isle of Wight Welcome

▶ Red Funnel's fast passenger ferry Red Jet 4 passes the Trinity House tender Galatea at the entrance to Cowes.

equitable lifestyle for inhabitants, most of whom settled on the Island to get away from modern life. This is partly achieved by concentrating much of the more commercial elements and development in a few coastal areas and getting on with life regardless. However, a constant tension exists between forces tending to turn the Island into a massive theme park and those seeking to preserve its unique character and community.

Even today, its diversity is its salvation, despite the fact that the Island subsists so much on tourism, and it is a mistake to see the Island community as a single entity.

There are considerable differences between the character of the coastal towns and that of the rural areas, between long established families and newcomers, even between Ryde and Cowes. A glance at the Isle of Wight County Press will show that thriving, vibrant communities (some of the parish churches are evidence of this) rub shoulders with less favoured areas.

For all that, the Islanders are a hardy, resilient bunch. The Garden Isle scarcely needs to sell itself in its present form and visitors are always afforded a warm welcome. There are constraints on growth if the Island is to maintain its fragile balance of commercialism, rural charm, unspoilt landscapes and community. A holiday or stay on the Island represents excellent value for money if the visitor enjoys the diversity of the Island's attractions, many of which are free, and perhaps limits the intensity of his or her, but more especially the children's, participation in the more blatantly commercial aspects.

About this guide

This guide has been arranged to take into account three main geographical areas on the Isle of Wight, which correspond to the ports of entry from the mainland. Therefore, we start with the eastern part of the Island, most readily accessible from Portsmouth through Fishbourne and Ryde, then the central part accessed from Southampton through Cowes and finally the west and Back of Wight, based on Yarmouth and the crossing from Lymington.

East Wight

Fishbourne To Ryde • Seaview to Bembridge • Vineyard Walk • Railways on the Isle of Wight • Palmerston's Solent Forts • Sandown • Shanklin • Shipwrecks •Ventnor • Inland

East Wight

The eastern part of the Island attracts most visitors because of its established coastal resorts, its communication network and, within its own terms, its extensive tourist infrastructure. As well as Ryde, the front-line seaside towns are Sandown, Shanklin and Ventnor, which, together with Brading and other satellites, offer attractions that appeal to a range of tastes and enthusiasms. It does get busy in the summer, but there are enough places to escape to, particularly in the hinterland, when the crowds get too much or the weather disappoints. A foot passenger arriving through Ryde or Fishbourne can easily move around eastern Wight and in season will find that he hardly needs a car to enjoy the rest of the Island, as transport links are easy to use.

Fishbourne To Ryde

Fishbourne Creek is dominated by the main Wightlink car ferry terminal. Home to the Royal Victoria Yacht Club, it is much frequented by yachtsmen. A short walk from Fishbourne and visible from the ferry are the distinctive towers of Quarr Abbey, built between 1908 and 1912. The spectacular red-brick Benedictine house, designed by Dom Paul Bellot, a pioneer of twentieth century Expressionism, was built as a permanent home for a community of displaced French monks from Solesmes, near Le Mans; today, they number about ten. The abbey church, in particular, is famous for its high pointed arches and windows.

The abbey church is open to the public, who are welcome to attend services, although it is advisable to phone in advance to check times (tel 01983 882420). Individuals who wish to get away from hectic lifestyles can volunteer for a retreat at Quarr. There is a book and gift shop adjacent to the Abbey and the Abbey Tea and Farm Shop is well worth a visit (quarrabbey.co.uk).

A little further on, in a field beside the footpath to Binstead and Ryde, is the site of the Cistercian abbey of Quarr, founded in 1132 by Baldwin de Redvers, originally as a Savignac house. It was once the leading religious institution on the Island and the pre-eminent place of burial for the local nobility.

► A Wightlink ferry berthed at Fishbourne.

18

During the Middle Ages, it acquired extensive lands, endowments and revenues, including numerous granges and farms on the Island.

Dissolved in 1536, much of the stone went to build the forts at Cowes and Yarmouth. Excavations in 1891 revealed the ground plan of the original monastery, but today all that remains above ground are a few isolated walls and a storehouse retained as a barn. Cottages nearby contain features made from salvaged materials.

Binstead church was founded in about 1170 apparently because the abbot of Quarr was fed up with the locals annoying the monks. Despite restoration in 1844 and a serious fire in 1969, many Early English features remain, together with the usual memorials and some interesting tombstones in the churchyard. There is also some fine panelling and stone carving and the grotesque Binstead 'idol' over a Norman archway in the south wall. From Binstead, a path through woodlands and past a golf course leads to a quiet beach.

A 1920s guidebook once said that Ryde was a town 'where no discriminating tourist will linger'. This is a mistake, for the town has much to offer. Ryde is the largest town on the Island, with a

▲ Isle of Wight footpaths.

▼ Quarr Abbey, a Benedictine monastery.

Quarr

Quarr derives its name from the nearby limestone quarries, originally worked by the Romans. The stone was used for the building of the old abbey, as well as the Norman cathedrals at Winchester and Chichester.

19

▲ Superbowl offers tenpin bowling and is part of the Pavilion on Ryde Esplanade.

population of 26,000, and indeed some visitors hardly venture beyond it, particularly the large number of day-trippers.

The town does have an air of faded Regency and Victorian grandeur and the atmosphere differs slightly from elsewhere on the Island. This may be because Portsmouth is clearly visible on the mainland, just a ten-minute hovercraft ride away. Also, Ryde has a very high level year-round residency and overall is less affected by seasonal changes in income and population.

Ryde comes from a local word, *ride* or *rithe*, meaning a small stream. There is archaeological and documentary evidence of continuity of settlement from the Neolithic period and late Bronze Age onwards. In medieval times, it was a fishing, trading and ferry settlement, but was burnt by the French in 1377. Subsequently, two settlements, Upper Ryde, along the High Street, and Lower Ryde, along the foreshore, grew up.

In 1780 Union Street was laid out by William Player to join the two communities and to create a Regency watering place to rival Brighton. By the late 1820s, fashionable Ryde was the most rapidly growing area of the Island, with increasing numbers of public buildings and rows of elegant houses. The Town Hall, St Thomas's Church and Brigstocke Terrace date from this period, to be followed by John Lind's classical assembly rooms and market in 1831 and Westmacott's Italianate Royal Victoria Arcade in 1836. Ryde's skyline is dominated by the 180ft (55m) spire of All Saints' church, a well-used seamark for ships entering and exiting Portsmouth. Sir George Gilbert Scott designed the predominantly alabaster and marble church to seat 1,300 souls. The spire was added in 1881-2.

The establishment of the Ryde to Ventnor railway line in the 1860s considerably opened up the resorts of the south-east coast and

Ryde

Farmers' Market

Ryde, Town Square, every Sat morning.

Ice Arena and Superbowl

Ryde PO33 2HH

On the Esplanade is the Planet Ice Arena and Skating Rink, which is open for recreational skating all year round and is home to the Wightlink Raiders ice hockey team. Tel 01983 615155

Next to the Ice Arena is Superbowl, a 22-lane bowling alley. Tel 01983 617070, www.rydesuperbowl.co.uk

Rosemary Vineyard

Smallbrook Lane PO33 4BE

Just south of Ryde. Open all year except Sun in winter. Tel 01983 811084. www.rosemaryvineyard.co.uk

Island Speedway at Smallbrook Stadium

Ashey Road, Ryde, PO33 4BH

Just south of Rosemary Vineyard. Weekly premier league speedway programme in the summer. Tel 01983 811180.

Waltzing Waters

Brading Road, Ryde PO33 1QS

A3055, Aqua Theatre at the Westridge Centre. Tel 01983 811333. www.waltzingwaters.co.uk

Ryde

Donald McGill Postcard Museum

15 Union Street, Ryde

Between 1904 and 1962 Donald McGill created over 12,000 saucy postcards and this small museum is dedicated to the King of the Seaside. Open 9.30am-4.30pm, Mon-Sat with last entry at 4pm. Open Sun in July & Aug. Entrance charge.

Orrery Cafe (address as above)

The award-winning Orrery Café has a working model of the solar system. Open 9.30am-4.30pm Mon-Sat, and Sun in Jul and Aug.

▲ Ryde Carnival Parade.

the growing popularity of Cowes led to the steady decline of Ryde as a fashionable resort in its own right. The pier, built in 1814, for ferry passengers, runs for half a mile (0.8km) into the sea and is the second longest in the country.

The first regular ferry service had been inaugurated in 1805 and the pier allowed travellers to disembark from ferries without the inconvenience of riding on a pony and cart across the muddy foreshore. 1817 saw the first steam ferry, but it was not until 1824

that a regular steamer service was instituted, taking thirty-four minutes. The landward end of the pier is the terminus for bus and coach services to other parts of the Island. The visitor cannot fail to see the assortment of hotels, guest houses, pubs, cafes, arcades and 'kiss me quick' souvenir shops.

The town with its outlying areas has six miles (9.6km) of sandy, clean beaches, which are ideal for swimming and, particularly at low tide, for playing. The long seafront esplanade is suitable for walks and there is a host of seasonal attractions, including putting,

▼ Appley Tower is a Victorian folly on the edge of the award-winning sands of Ryde beach. It is now home to a small crystal and rune shop, and visitors can climb to the top of the tower for views across the Solent.

East Wight

trampolines, a marina and a canoe lake. In a field by the Esplanade, now the boating lake, the victims of the wreck of the *Royal George*, the flagship of Admiral Kempenfelt, were buried in 1782. Wives and families were on board when she sank in Spithead and at least 800 souls perished. There is a small memorial to the *Royal George* opposite Esplanade Gardens.

On the eastern side of Ryde is Appley Park, formerly a private estate built by a blacksmith called Boyce, who was suspected of making his money in smuggling. It has ornamental gardens, woods and a pitch and putt. Further along the coast Puckpool Park stands on the site of a former battery. Now it is a well-laid out park, with a bowling green, tennis courts, mini golf, putting green, swings and a play area. There are also an aquarium, an aviary and some quiet wooded walks.

Shopping in Ryde requires an element of exploration. Union Street, once full of elegant townhouses, but now housing traditional and more unusual shops, runs from the Esplanade into the High Street and beyond. Half way up Union Street on the right hand side is the Royal Victoria Arcade, saved by conservationists in the 1970s. One can detect its former grandeur when looking up at the ceiling, but the shops do not match its nineteenth century glory. It is full of bric-a-brac, clothes and alternative shops, some of which are worth a browse.

Just off Union Street at its junction with the High Street is St Thomas's Church. Built in 1827, it no longer functions as a church, but you can sit down and contemplate your surroundings in the former churchyard which is now a 'rest' garden. There is a First Fleet (to Australia) bi-centenary memorial close to the church unveiled by HM The Queen in 1987. Further up the High Street, there is a regular Farmers Market in Ryde Town Square on Saturday mornings. Through the main shopping precinct is St Mary's Roman Catholic church. Built in early

English style, it was designed by Joseph Hansom, the creator of the Hansom Cab, in 1844-46.

Ryde Theatre on Lind Street stands on the site of an old theatre. Here, Mrs Jordan appeared for the last time in England and Ellen Terry, as a child, for the first time, playing Puck in *A Midsummer Night's Dream*. On the outskirts of Ryde is Waltzing Waters, a forty-minute show with moving fountains and waterspouts synchronised with waltzes and music. Close by, is the Busy Bee Garden Centre with the Honeypot coffee shop (tel 01983 811096).

Rosemary Vineyard is on a thirty-acre (twelve-hectare) site that was planted in 1986 at 60ft (18m) above sea level. There are tours and tastings available and a small shop selling wine and other related products. The Vine Leaf is open for snacks. In fine weather, visitors can follow the sign-posted vineyard trail. Smallbrook railway junction is located nearby and

PLACES TO VISIT

Seaview

Seaview Wildlife Encounter
(formerly Flamingo Park)
Springvale, Seaview PO34 5AP
Open April to October, daily, 10am–5pm. 10am–4pm daily in Oct. Tel 01983 612153
www.seaviewwildlife.com

is the interchange for the main railway line. **NB** It is not possible to join trains here, except by the Isle of Wight Steam Railway.

Seaview to Bembridge

The quieter and more exclusive resort of Seaview is about 2.5 miles (4km) east of Ryde, along the Duver Road. The sea-front provides uninterrupted and extensive views of Spithead, the shipping activity in the Solent and the scenery of the mainland. It is a popular summer sailing centre and there are two sandy bays suitable for bathing in water that is distinctly clear. Close to Priory Bay, beyond Horestone Point, and Nettlestone are less busy

◀ Built around 1700, Bembridge windmill last operated in 1913 but still has most of its original machinery intact.

East Wight

Vineyard Walk

Distance: approximately 5 miles (8km)

The close proximity of two of the three main Island vineyards – Rosemary and Adgestone – offers the opportunity to base a walk on the vineyard theme. Start at Ryde St John's station and take the Nunwell Trail (follow the red flashes on the signposts) through the suburb of Oakfield. Go along the railway and just north of Smallbrook Junction, turn right over the railway and take Smallbrook Lane to Rosemary Vineyard. Leaving the vineyard, turn right and continue up the lane, passing a stadium on your left. Turn left at the crossroads onto Ashey Road and pick up the trail again leading off to the left after about 550 yds (500 m). Continue across open country until you hit a small road near Hardingshute Farm and turn right. Cross West Lane and walk towards Nunwell Farm, with Nunwell House visible to your left. Take a sharp right turn, skirting a small wood, then – particular care is needed here – turn sharp left, leaving the Nunwell trail, onto a bridlepath. After about 220 yards (200m) fork right and ascend Brading Down for a wonderful view to the south. Descend into Adgestone and the vineyard is on your right as you hit the first minor road. To return to Ryde St John's, walk along the Lower Adgestone Road towards the Yarbridge crossroads and pick up the footpath on the east side of the railway. Follow this to Brading station and catch the train.

and St Helen's can be reached along the sands at low tide.

The nearby Seaview Wildlife Encounter is home to a large number of rare and beautiful birds and animals, as well as the famous flamingos and critically endangered Humboldt penguins. It is also a fascinating wildlife experience with mammal species from around the world, including wallabies and meerkats and one of the largest tropical aviaries in the UK. There is a gift shop, café and water displays.

In the area are many footpaths and two extremely pleasant walking routes along the coast. One goes to Ryde, initially along the Duver Road to Puckpool Park and then along the sands (at low tide) or along the sea-wall.

The other takes the Coastal Path which weaves inland to St Helen's and takes in the Duver, a spit of sand and shingle projecting into Bembridge Harbour.

St Helen's is a scattered village grouped loosely around an open green. In medieval times, a Cluniac Priory stood near the old church. Only part of the square tower of this church remains as a sea-mark and a new church of 1717 was constructed on the road to Nettlestone.

In the late eighteenth century the village, with a population of 2,000, thrived as a supply port for sailing men-of-war, which lay offshore in St Helen's Roads to avoid being trapped in Spithead or Portsmouth by adverse winds. It was also a good place to ensure pressed men did not desert and, sheltered from the westerly winds, to conduct gunnery and sail handling training. Stones from the old church were used to scrape the dirt and salt off the upper decks of the ships, hence the expression 'holystoning', or polishing, the decks. Offshore is St Helen's Fort, one of Palmerston's artillery forts

◀ Seaview is a picturesque small village, about two miles from Ryde. It is extremely popular with families who holiday here year after year.

of 1860, to which an annual walk takes place at low tide.

Bembridge Down offers one of the best and most varied views on the Island, from the Hampshire coast all the way round to Dunnose Head, with Bembridge in the foreground. Next to the easterly car park, there is an obelisk commemorating the first Earl of Yarborough, who was the first Commodore of the Royal Yacht Squadron. He paid his yachting crews extra wages if they would voluntarily conform to the regulations of the Royal Navy; at that time, these included flogging for various infractions of discipline.

Culver Cliff (National Trust), a striking mass of chalk and flint, defines the northern end of Sandown Bay and fronts Bembridge Down. From the northern end of Sandown seafront, it can be reached by a cliff path on foot and the return trip is about five miles (8km). Others may wish to walk along the sands at the base of the cliffs, at appropriate levels of tide, and enjoy the foreshore and rock pools. The cliff is approachable by road through Yaverland by continuing beyond the fort on the summit of Bembridge Down.

Bembridge and St Helens used to be situated on either side of the entrance to Brading Haven and Bembridge itself was virtually cut off from the rest of the Island.

▼ The new lifeboat station at Bembridge was completed in 2011.

Railways on the Isle of Wight

Visitors will see on maps and on the ground that the Island was once covered with an extensive railway network. The first line was started in 1859 from Cowes to Newport and by 1900 there were 55 miles (89km) of track, with an extension to Ryde Pier Head to connect with the ferries. In the 1930s, on each Saturday in summer, 36,000 passengers would pass through Ryde Pier and a train would leave every ten minutes.

After nationalisation in 1948 and increasing competition from road transport, the branch lines ceased to be economic and by 1960 all but the 8.5-mile (13.6km) section between Ryde Pier Head and Shanklin had been shut. Since 1966 the service has been modernized using electrified ex-

IOW Steam Railway.

Underground stock. The line – the Island Line – was officially recognised as Britain's most punctual and reliable rail service.

The small village of Havenstreet was a haven when Wootton Creek extended further inland. Today, it is the headquarters and maintenance depot of the Isle of Wight Steam Railway, which operates a 5.2-mile (8.3km) line between Wootton and Smallbrook Junction, with intermediate stations at Havenstreet and Ashey, principally with the support of volunteers.

After the last steam service on the Island came to an end, a group of enthusiasts formed the Wight Locomotive Society in 1966 to preserve one of the surviving locomotives. The two-mile (3.2km) stretch of track between Wootton and Havenstreet was leased from 1971 and acquisitions of locomotives, rolling stock and buildings from all over the Island since then have subtained rapid development.

Nowadays, the line connects at Smallbrook Junction with the Island Line and regular passenger and themed services are operated along the whole preserved section, using a combination of Victorian, Edwardian and younger engines and carriages. Trains run about every hour during the day in

Eventually, a mile long embankment was built from St Helens to Bembridge to keep out the sea. A railway link was founded and the village, supposedly the largest in the country, grew in size and popularity.

Bembridge is today a trendy yachting and residential area. The rim of today's shallow haven is fronted with houseboats and other nautical paraphernalia. The prestigious Bembridge Sailing Club, founded in 1886, has an interesting traditional clubhouse fronting the sea along the embankment. Bembridge is in fact home to two

sailing clubs – the other is the Brading Haven Yacht Club – and both clubs host sailing activities all year round. A busy marina is operated at St Helen's and a number of fishing craft work out of the harbour; fishing trips can be booked.

The newly-built impressive RNLI lifeboat station at Lane End operates a Tamar all-weather and a D class inshore lifeboat. The lifeboat station is usually open to the public during the summer for free guided tours, subject to operational requirements.

Bembridge village has a variety of shops, pubs and restaurants.

summer and the rural stations themselves are delightful and very evocative, having incorporated structures rescued from other long lost stations on the Island (see www.iwsteamrailway.co.uk).

Real enthusiasts wishing to explore the old tracks should start at Havenstreet Station itself where there are a well-stocked souvenir and railway memorabilia shop and an interesting collection of local railway items. It is also the best place to see the engines and rolling stock, although visits to the depot itself are not permitted. Visitors can gain an appreciation of the network at its height and an understanding of its history. Nearby, Ashey is a good place for ramblers and cyclists to alight, by request, but it is not accessible by car. Similarly, access at Smallbrook Junction is only by rail.

The Ryde Bookshop in the High Street specialises in railways and transport with a wide range of publications about the Isle of Wight network (tel 01983 565227). There are four short walks, which take in the old railway track beds and which are clearly marked on the Ordnance Survey Outdoor Leisure Map 29.

- **Cowes to Newport (4.5 miles/7.2km)** This popular route starts at the end of Arctic Road, Cowes, and runs along the west bank of the Medina. It has a layer of tarmac, making it suitable for walkers, cyclists and wheelchairs.

- **Yarmouth to Freshwater (2.5 miles/4km)** This is a wonderful walk along the eastern bank of the River Yar, returning to Yarmouth on the western side or continuing into Freshwater itself.
- **Shanklin to Wroxall (2.5 miles/4km)** This walk starts south of Shanklin station and winds around St Martin's Down. A picturesque and rewarding return is easily made along the Worsley Trail from Wroxall.
- **Sandown to Horringford (3 miles/4.8km)** Start at Sandown station and follow the Nunwell trail along Golf Links Road and Longwood road 880yds/800m to some reservoirs. Here the old track bed is visible as a path heading off to the left alongside the golf course. The path heads via Alverstone to Horringford.

▲ One of the 1938-built former London tube trains which have been on the Island since 1989.

Well worth a visit is the Bembridge Heritage Centre, which houses a fascinating exhibition of items collected by the Heritage Society and its members. Located at the back of the library building, one of the exhibition displays is a restored Operation PLUTO pump, used in Sandown to pump petrol across the Channel in 1944 following D-Day. Two films describe the restoration and how the pump was used. Other displays cover the airport, Britten-Norman aircraft and the railway.

Just outside the village is the last remaining windmill on the Island that dates from 1700 and commands spectacular views of the surrounding countryside. Bembridge Windmill (National Trust) has been restored and contains a complete set of wooden machinery and gearing, most of which is original. Bembridge Airport has the only all-weather runway and facilities on the Island.

From Bembridge Point, there is a remarkable sea view and at low tide a long stretch of firm sand, ideal for children and adults. Under Tyne with its sand and shingle is the only place to bathe. There is a cheerful, scenic coast walk from Bembridge to

East Wight

PLACES TO VISIT

St Helens

Oasis

Carpenter's Road, St Helens
PO36 0QA
Unusual shop, full of knickknacks
sourced from all over the world.
Tel 01983 613760
www.oasis-iow.co.uk

Sandown (five miles/8km), via the Foreland, Whitecliff Bay, Culver Cliff and Bembridge Down.

Brading used to send two members to Parliament, but has been left high and dry, both by history and by reclamation of the once navigable Brading Haven in 1878. Today, it is easy for travellers to miss Brading, but it is worth stopping. There are several attractions, not least the church, a line of old cottages (most with nineteenth-century frontages) in the High Street, and the water meadows along the river Yar.

Quay Lane, which lies between the church and the former wax museum, gives access to the water meadows and an excellent walk to Bembridge, via its windmill.

Brading is also a convenient centre for walking the Downs, with easy access to Brading, Ashey, Mersley and Arreton Downs and elsewhere, all at an altitude of between 300 and 400ft (92m and 122m).

A Saxon church may have stood on the site of St Mary's, but the current church dates from 1150-1250. It has a host of interesting features: a tower built on piers, a thirteenth-century font, the Oglander and de Aula family chapels and evocative stained glass.

The Oglander table-tombs and memorials, commemorating probably the most notable Island family, from nearby Nunwell, are remarkable, including one with a 'Pieta' by Francia. Next to the church is the Old Town Hall which houses stocks and a whipping post.

The village lock-up was also in the building. Opposite it is the former rectory dating back to 1600 or earlier, for many years part of Brading Wax Museum and Experience, which has now closed.

Brading Roman Villa stands on what once was one of the inlets

▼ St Helen's Fort can be seen from Bembridge.

28

◀ Sandown Bay extends for more than six miles from Culver Cliff to just south of Shanklin.

formed by Brading Haven and was probably a major agricultural centre of production. It has been plausibly associated with the breakaway Empire of Carausius and Allectus in the third century. Considered one of the finest Romano-British archaeological sites in the UK, the villa existed for most of the Roman era in Britain, before being abandoned in the fifth century. The excellent, modern museum and visitor centre house the remains of the main rooms of a substantial house with detailed mosaics depicting scenes of Roman fables and themes that reflect the wealth and cultural background of the occupants. The car park area is a great place for a picnic close to the sites of extensive Roman outbuildings uncovered by the

Palmerston's Solent Forts

A series of forts were built to defend the Solent and Portsmouth and command the area's strategic shipping channels The four forts that can be seen in the Solent were built in the 1860s to defend Portsmouth and the Solent against possible attack. During the Crimean war the Royal Navy had been surprised by the effectiveness of the Russian forts at Sebastopol, so plans for fortifications at key ports and points along the south and east coasts of England were drafted.

As Britain's pre-eminent naval port, it was considered that Portsmouth needed an all round defence, and a comprehensive system of forts and artillery batteries was built in the 1860s around Gosport, Portsmouth and the Isle of Wight to strengthen existing arrangements at a cost of about £1.5 million.

The four Solent sea forts were built to cover the deep-water passage through Spithead. The two largest are No Man's Land and Horse Sand, with the smaller, Spitbank and St Helen's, and were all constructed 1868-71 with a complex layered structure of armour and heavy masonry on granite foundations. Other forts in the system can be seen at intervals along the crest of Portsdown Hill above Portsmouth.

Around the Island, other traces of the system may be seen, particularly guarding the Needles' Channel (Fort Victoria, Fort Albert, Golden Hill and a host of minor batteries on the Freshwater Peninsula) and at Sandown, Bembridge, Yaverland and Puckpool, protecting the eastern approaches to the Island.

▶ The village of Brading contains some of the oldest buildings on the Island.

2008 excavations and the well holds a sinister secret.

Close by is the privately owned Morton Manor. Brading Station is within walking distance where the old waiting room has been refurbished as a Railway Heritage and Visitors Centre, which is usually open every day 11am-3pm.

Yaverland lies between Brading and Sandown. The church was built in about 1150 as a chapel of the de Aula family, which owned the manor house at a time when Yaverland was a tidal island. It became a parish church in the fifteenth century and was heavily restored in 1889. However, many of its original, particularly Norman, features have been retained. The privately owned Jacobean Manor House is not open to the public.

Sandown

Sitting in its six-mile (10km) wide bay, between the chalk of Culver Cliff and the ruddy Dunnose Head, Sandown is one of the Island's premier holiday resorts. The red brick town is somewhat overpopulated with hotels and guesthouses, but it has a wonderful sandy beach, unencumbered by rocks and pebbles, and a pier. It does get very busy in season and is especially geared for entertaining families and children. Like many busy seasonal resorts, it can look rather run down and distinctly sad in the winter.

Sandown shares the bay with its posher neighbour, Shanklin, together with a sheltered south-easterly aspect and the sunshine record for the south of England. Indeed, they are administratively

---

PLACES TO VISIT

Brading

Adgestone Vineyard
Near Brading PO36 0ES
Annually produces up to 20 000 bottles of white, rosé, red and sprakling wine, mostly using German grape varieties. Small shop, café and tasting room plus b&b. Open Easter to Oct, daily, 10am–5.30pm. Limited winter opening. Tel 01983 402503, adgestonevineyard.co.uk

Brading Roman Villa
Morton Old Road, Brading PO36 0EN
Open all year (except Christmas) 9.30am–5pm. Last entry at 4pm. Coffee shop open daily. Tel 01983 406223, www.bradingromanvilla.org.uk

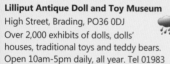

| 7 | 12 |
| 45 | 90 |

Lilliput Antique Doll and Toy Museum
High Street, Brading, PO36 0DJ
Over 2,000 exhibits of dolls, dolls' houses, traditional toys and teddy bears. Open 10am-5pm daily, all year. Tel 01983 407231. www.lilliputmuseum.org.uk

| 7 | 12 |
| 60 | 60 |

Nunwell House
PO36 0JQ
A mile west of Brading is the former seat of the Oglander family at least since the reign of Henry I (1100-1135). This Jacobean and Georgian building has a collection of period furniture. House and Garden open July-Sept, Mon, Tue & Wed afternoons. Ring to check. Garden may open at other times for charity. Tel 01983 407240

and psychologically linked; even in 1920, Ward Lock's guide book observed, 'The twin towns of Sandown and Shanklin share this bay between them. There is every indication that their rivalry will one day cease by the simple process of amalgamation'.

In 1537 Sir Richard Worsley of Appuldurcombe, Captain of the Island, built a castle at Sandham on behalf of Henry VIII to protect the vulnerable east coast from invaders. This fort fell into the sea in about 1630 and a successor was demolished in the nineteenth-century. In 1861, work began on a new Sandown fort, which was complete by 1866, but is now the Isle of Wight Zoo.

The town's popularity grew as a resort in company with Shanklin and Ventnor during the mid-Victorian era, particularly after the construction of the railway from Ryde and after 1867 when Dr Henry Maund extolled the virtues of the air and low mortality rate. Lodging houses proliferated and in 1874 four European monarchs

stayed (ironically, the same year that Karl Marx stayed in Ventnor).

Sandown Pier first opened in 1878 and is 1,000ft (305m) long, having been lengthened in 1895 and a landing stage added

PLACES TO VISIT

Sandown

Dinosaur Isle
Culver Par. PO36 8QA
Interactive Dinosaur and Geology Museum.
Open daily, all year, Nov to Mar 10am–4pm (last entry 3pm); Apr to Aug 10am–6pm and 5pm in Sept & Oct (last entry 5pm and 4pm in Oct). Closed 24, 25 & 26 Dec & 1 Jan. Tel 01983 404344, www.dinosaurisle.com

Sandown Pier
Bowling, adventure golf and children's play area. Open daily, 9am–10pm. Tel 01983 404122

The Isle of Wight Zoo
Yaverland Seafront,
Sandown PO36 8QB
Facilities include a large car park, gift shop and snack bar. Open Apr-Sept, 10am-6pm, and mid-Feb to March and Oct, daily 10am–4pm. Tel 01983 403883.
www.isleofwightzoo.com

▼ Brading Roman Villa is one of the finest Romano-British archaeological sites in the UK.

East Wight

▲ Dinosaur Isle, Britain's first purpose-built dinosaur museum.

to give access by steamer. The large pier pavilion was built at a cost of £26,000 in 1934 and now houses an all year round entertainment complex. The view from the seaward end of the pier is exhilarating. The esplanade is well supplied with bars, cafés, bingo halls and amusement arcades and Sunday is market day in Sandown.

At the Yaverland end of the town are long and short pitch and putt courses (Brown's) plus the famous zoo housed in Granite Fort. At the northern end of the esplanade are Sandham Grounds, home to a variety of amusements including putting, tennis and bowls.

Famous Visitors

Charles Darwin began writing the work popularly known as 'The Origin of Species' in Sandown, and Sir Isaac Pitman formulated his famous system of shorthand there. Lewis Carroll, John Keats, George Eliot and Henry Longfellow were also appreciative visitors.

Nearby is an eighteen-inch (46cm) deep canoe lake. The Isle of Wight Zoo houses tigers, lions and jaguars. There are many other exotic species, such as lemurs, monkeys, reptiles, birds, insects and giant spiders.

In 2001 a brand new all weather, purpose built interactive attraction known as Dinosaur Isle opened on Culver Parade and incorporated the geology museum previously located in Sandown library. Life-size dinosaur models are featured in their natural landscape as well as a display of fossils found on the Isle of Wight. At the southern end of the esplanade is a clifftop walk to Shanklin with access to Battery Gardens on the site of an old fortlet.

Lake is a residential area sandwiched between Sandown and Shanklin struggling to retain its identity. An early twentieth century visitor noted gloomily, 'Lake, nearly midway between Sandown and

Shipwrecks

In 1878, the passage of the 900-ton, twenty-six-gun frigate Eurydice on her return from a West Indies training cruise was witnessed by the four-year-old Winston Churchill and his nurse, who hurried home to avoid a storm. The ship subsequently went down in a squall in the same storm and, of the 300 crew, only two were saved. Seven of the drowned were buried in the churchyard of Christ Church, Sandown. A memorial reads, "Sacred to the memory of seven brave men of Her Majesty's Navy, who lie buried here after having first found a watery grave on Sunday 24 March 1878 when HMS Eurydice foundered in a terrific squall off Sandown Bay".

Shanklin, already affords a link and it will soon be difficult for the stranger to say where Sandown ends and Shanklin begins'.

Shanklin

The old village of Shanklin, with its thatched cottages and 400-year old Crab Inn, was built at the top of a chine, which winds from the 100ft (30.5m) cliff-top to the sea, and to the south of the present town. The church, another of Norman origin, had virtually a complete makeover in 1852 and was significantly extended. There is a variety of souvenir and gift shops while walkers will find paths radiating inland and up on to the Downs.

In 1545 the Shanklin Chine was the scene of a battle to repel French raiders, during which their commander was killed. It now contains waterfalls, trees and lush vegetation to which footpaths and walkways allow access for visitors. A Heritage Centre tells the history of the Chine in words and pictures.

To the south is Rylstone Gardens, a well-tended and picturesque location with lawns, conifers and shrubs. The views are extensive and the gardens lead to Appley Green and the beach.

The esplanade and a sandy beach tend to be, but are not always, quieter than Sandown. There is a lift between the cliff top and the sea front. It has a putting green, crazy golf and the usual run of amusements, arcades and children's temptations. For adults, there is a broad selection of pubs, eateries and restaurants, as well as live entertainment in season. Shanklin Theatre has up to eight different shows per week in the high season.

From the old church, a well marked path leads to Shanklin Down and then St Boniface Down, at 783ft (239m) the highest point on the Island, and the pleasant, climb is worth the effort. Another walk, over three miles (4.8km), to Ventnor, takes in Luccombe Chine, the Landslip and Bonchurch.

Once in Luccombe, there is a pleasant walk to Luccombe Common and Nansen Hill, from which there is an extensive view of Sandown Bay. A further walk extends to Luccombe Chine, which as far as Dunnose Head gives access to the Landslip. This is a well-signed jumble of rocks and vegetation with footpaths and routes of varying difficulty, ideal for

▼ The obelisk erected in memory of Earl Yarborough (1780-1846) was constructed in 1848-9 and can be seen at Culver Down, Bembridge.

▲ The picturesque village of old Shanklin.

Shanklin

Shanklin Chine
Shanklin, Esplanade PO37 6BW or
Shanklin, Old Village PO37 6QT
Open Easter to late-May and
mid-Sept to end-Oct, daily,
10am–5pm. Late-May to mid-
Sept, daily, 10am–10pm. Open
subject to weather conditions.
Tel 01983 866432
www.shanklinchine.co.uk

Shanklin Theatre
Prospect Rd, Shanklin PO37 6AJ
Tel 01983 868000
www.shanklintheatre.com

exploring and for getting down to the caves of Luccombe and Monks Bay. The more adventurous can enjoy a scramble down the steps of the Devil's Chimney and other clefts; others might prefer the gardens on the Upper Landslip.

Shanklin's pier was severely damaged in the hurricane of 1987 and after further deterioration was demolished in 1993. It had been the base for PLUTO, the Pipe Line Under The Ocean, which supplied fuel oil to the Allied Expeditionary Force for the 1944 D-Day landings.

Ventnor

Ventnor has merged with the older village of Bonchurch which still retains some charm with its pond and church. At its centre is a remarkable shrub and tree-lined pond, which was given to the village as a memorial to his wife by H de Vere Stacpoole, author of *The Blue Lagoon* and the poem, *In*

▶ Shanklin Theatre remains open throughout the year hosting events ranging from a Christmas Pantomime and a professional summer season to local amateur dramatics and the IOW Dance Festival.

a Bonchurch Garden. He was one of many members of Victorian society who chose to live in Bonchurch, including Tennyson, Macaulay, and Elisabeth Sewell.

The charming, simple old church of St Boniface, peacefully set among trees and roses, was probably built around 1070 on a site of early Saxon foundation. Houses nearby also have their literary associations: the poet Swinburne was born at East Dene and Dickens lived for a while at Winterbourne, writing part of *David Copperfield* here. Swinburne is buried along with other members of his family at the newer church of St Boniface, built in 1847-8.

Facing south and in a sheltered position, Ventnor grew rapidly as a health resort in the 1840s, as visitors sought to take advantage of the mild winter climate and sea air. On a one in four incline to a height of 800ft (244m), it is built on a series of terraces, which have been likened by some to rows of seats in a theatre. These are supplemented by flights of stairs and zig-zag roads which may deter all but the most determined explorer on foot.

Its major buildings and numerous churches all date from the mid-Victorian era and there are antique and other interesting shops. Ventnor has many of the attractions associated with the modern tourist expectations, most of which are close to sea level, but the quaintness of the town prevents this aspect becoming overpowering. A Victorian style bandstand has been built where the old pier stood and evening concerts take place in the summer. Ventnor's sea-front is divided by a 'cascade'. On the eastern side, there is a canoe lake, paddling pool and a promenade with gardens and the usual amenities. The western portion is dominated by a beach, which is sand and fine shingle with some rocky outcrops.

Local sightseeing and charter fishing trips (www.

▲ Ventnor from the sea. Its upper part offers probably one of the best views on the Island.

East Wight

▲ Ventnor, a Victorian seaside town on the southern side of the Island.

oceanblueseacharters. co.uk) depart from Ventnor Haven which opened in 2003. It provides the only stopping off point for yachts and motor boats on the south coast of the Isle of Wight. Fresh fish is available daily from the newly-built fish wharf above the Haven. The family firm of Blake has fished from the beach for five generations and still sells to local restaurants and pubs.

One of Ventnor's most attractive and popular features is its Park, which takes up most of its southern slope. Amid the plants and paths, there is enough space for visitors to enjoy privacy while appreciating the commanding views.

The Undercliff, a seven-mile (11.2km) long landslip, forms a remarkable inland cliff about 600yds (550m) wide between

PLACES TO VISIT

Ventnor

Botanic Gardens
Undercliff Dr, Ventnor
PO38 1UL
Open during daylight hours all year; has a cafe. Tel 01983 855397. www.botanic.co.uk

Isle of Wight Studio Glass
St Lawrence, PO38 1XR
Open Oct to Easter, Mon to Fri 10am–4pm. Easter to Oct, daily, 9am–5pm. Closed Christmas Holiday period. Tel 01983 853526
www.isleofwightstudioglass.co.uk

Longshoreman's Museum
The Esplanade PO38 1JT
Ventnor's nautical history with photos, engravings and models.
Tel 01983 853176

Ventnor Heritage Centre & Local History Museum
11 Spring Hill, Ventnor PO38 1PE
Tel 01983 855407
www.ventnorheritage.org.uk

Blackgang and Luccombe. Recurrent slides and falls have been caused by the unusual geological structure, the action of weather and the presence of numerous streams. The main culprit is the combination of chalk and greensand layers overlying the 'Blue Slipper' clay.

Most significant activity occurred in prehistoric times, but there have been memorable slips in 1799, 1818 and in 1928, when a major section of the coast road was lost. In February 1995 1.5 million tonnes of rock and debris crashed into the sea between Bonchurch and Dunnose.

The whole area is rich in plants and vegetation, providing a ready habitat for birds and other local wildlife. It is also a favourite stopover for migrating species. Numerous paths give access along its whole length and exploration is highly recommended for adults and children, particularly the uninterrupted stretch between the

Botanic Gardens and Blackgang (five miles/8km).

The Botanic Gardens, which benefit from the sub-tropical climatic of Ventnor's situation, contain over 10,000 plants and 4,000 species, some of which might seem more at home in a Mediterranean environment. Formerly the site of the Royal National Hospital for Diseases of the Chest founded in 1861, the twenty-two-acre (nine-hectare) gardens are located on the terraces

▲ Ventnor seafront.

◀ Ventnor from the western end of the seafront.

PLACES TO VISIT

Newchurch
Amazon World
Watery Ln, Newchurch
PO36 OLX

Includes animal enclosures
and children's play area.
Open all year. Tel 01983 867122,
www.amazonworld.co.uk

Shared Earth next to Amazon
World – Fair Trade Gift Shopping.
Tel 01983 718223

Garlic Farm Shop and Café
Newchurch PO36 0NR
Open daily, all year. Tel 01983
867333. www.the garlicfarm.co.uk

▲ Bonchurch Pond is home to carp, which rise up when visitors throw them bread.

of the former hospital grounds.

St Lawrence is part of the ribbon development south-west of Ventnor and can be reached along the main road or the Undercliff. The tiny, evocative church is off the beaten track and set in woods, but fully repays the effort of a visit. It dates from the twelfth century and originally measured only 25ft by 11ft by 6ft (7.6m x 3.4m x 1.8m) high (up to its beams). Until 1842, when a new chancel extended its length by 15ft (4.6m), it was the smallest parish church in England.

A newer church designed by Gilbert Scott, built in 1878, has pre-Raphaelite stained glass salvaged from the Royal National Hospital.

Nearby is Lisle Combe, bought by the poet Alfred Noyes in the Thirties. It is still owned by his family and run as a farmhouse B&B (www. lislecombe. co.uk). Guests have access to the adjacent farm.

Close to St Lawrence Undercliff, in a converted farm building, is the internationally renowned studio of Isle of Wight Studio Glass where glassmaking is demonstrated.

Inland

Newchurch, with its panoramic views on the end of a long escarpment, retains a rural, attractive atmosphere and stands above the eastern Yar river valley. Its church, dating from Norman times and containing a number of curiosities, principally a tower clad in eighteenth-century weather boarding, has the best view of all.

The village has long been the centre of the Island's horticulture and today has several nurseries and garden centres. More recently, garlic, asparagus and sweetcorn

Donkey Sanctuary

On the outskirts of Wroxall, on the road to Godshill, is the Isle of Wight Donkey Sanctuary. Over 200 donkeys have been rescued and given a permanent home by a registered charity that subsists entirely on voluntary donations. The Sanctuary was established in 1987 to provide any donkey in distress or in need of care and attention, a safe and permanent home.

have been farmed and an annual two-day garlic festival takes place on the third weekend in August (see www.garlic-festival.co.uk).

Newchurch has good connections and opportunities for walking and cycling with many footpaths, bridleways and cycle tracks. Wildlife enthusiasts will be able to visit the nearby Alverstone Nature Reserve, which has red squirrels. Alverstone itself has an old mill and some pleasant cottages, with opportunities for refreshments.

Just to the south is Queen's Bower, where there is access to Borthwood Copse, whose paths thread through quiet and dense woodland, thickly set with wild flowers. A further walk to Brading Down (near Adgestone Vineyard) allows a stroll along a butterfly footpath where the Glanville fritillary butterfly, unique to the Island, can be found.

Amazon World, adjacent to Thompson's Café, Plant and Garden Centre, is a great all weather

◀ Newchurch obtained its name from the new church built in 1087 by Norman monks.

attraction, as well as being an enjoyable educational experience. Exotic birds fly freely among the lush tropical growth where marmosets and monkeys play. Amazon World recreates the story of the rainforest and portrays the environment of endangered species and life in the jungle.

Wroxall's hitherto agricultural character was transformed by the railway, which Lord Yarborough of Appuldurcombe would not allow across his land. Consequently, a tunnel of 1,301 yards (1,190m) was

▼ Even as a shell, Appuldurcombe House is one of the grandest and most striking houses on the island.

► The village of Newchurch is located between Sandown and Newport.

cut through St Boniface Down and Wroxall's cottages were expanded to house the workers.

The village, in a hollow of the Downs, has walks in all directions. Wroxall's main attraction is Appuldurcombe House, a partly roofless, but impressive shell with grounds landscaped by Capability Brown. Its history mainly revolves around the Worsley family, which came from Lancashire. James Worsley was a page to King

Henry VII and a companion to the future King Henry VIII. In 1509 Worsley was knighted and made Captain of the Isle of Wight. He married Ann Leigh, the heiress of Appuldurcombe, and founded a dynasty which dominated Island politics and life for three centuries.

The original house was demolished and a Palladian mansion of 1701 built in its place. In 1855, when the estate was sold, the house became successively a hotel, a school and finally a temporary refuge for Benedictine monks during the building of Quarr Abbey. From 1909, it decayed rapidly and today it is maintained by English Heritage.

Whitwell, behind St Lawrence, is remarkable for the double-naved church of St Mary and St Rhadegund that has been formed by the incorporation of two medieval chapels built exactly side by side by different lords. Nearby, Nettlecombe Farm (tel 01983 730783) has three commercial lakes for coarse angling.

PLACES TO VISIT

Wroxall

Appuldurcombe House
Wroxall PO38 3EW

An Owl and Falconry Centre in the laundry and brewhouse with regular flying displays. Open April to mid-October, daily, 10am–4pm. Tel 01983 852484
www.appuldurcombe.co.uk

Isle of Wight Donkey Sanctuary
St Johns Road,
Wroxall PO38 3AA

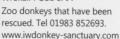

Zoo donkeys that have been rescued. Tel 01983 852693.
www.iwdonkey-sanctuary.com

The Centre of the Island

Cowes • Around the Medina • Sailing Legend • Osborne House • IOW Lavender • Ghosts • Newport • Charles I and Carisbrooke Castle • Old Gallows • Further South • Godshill

The Centre of the Island

The central part of the Island is dominated by the valley of the Medina, with Cowes at its mouth, and the pivotal position of the island's administrative capital, Newport. Its historic significance is emphasised by the site of the key royal castle of Carisbrooke and the legacy of the Victorian era centred on Osborne House.

The influence and involvement of Queen Victoria are everywhere apparent, from memorials by loyal subjects to personal initiatives by the Queen-Empress herself in the life and character of the community. Further south, and stretching to St Catherine's Point, are unspoilt villages, open downland and spectacular views.

Cowes

Comprising East and West Cowes, linked by a regular floating chain bridge across the Medina estuary (which takes cars), Cowes lives off its reputation as one of the world's top yachting venues, in particular the prestige associated with the annual 'Cowes Week', and as the home of the Royal Yacht Squadron. Facing directly onto Southampton Water, it is also the entry port for visitors arriving from Southampton.

The first recorded use of the name 'Cows' was in 1414 and possibly referred to two sandbanks, which lay off the mouth of the Medina. However, a settlement had existed at East Cowes at least from the thirteenth century, and, a century later (with the name of Shamblord), this was one of the three main recognised ports of the Island. Its importance as a roadstead and harbour was such that Henry VIII built two forts on either side of the mouth of the river to guard the haven and protect the Island's northern coastline. (Interestingly, the Tudor word for a fortified emplacement was a cow.) East Cowes Castle no longer exists, but West Cowes castle has been incorporated into the headquarters of the Royal Yacht Squadron.

By the eighteenth century, shipbuilding, trade and the fashionable pursuit of sea-bathing

▼ Boat trips and harbour tours on the river Medina from Cowes.

Yachting at Cowes

The first attested race at Cowes took place in 1788 and, after the Royal Yacht Club was formed in 1815 in London, its first organised events were held in 1826. The Club moved to Cowes in 1854, having adopted the title Royal Yacht Squadron in 1833, under the patronage of William IV. The Prince of Wales (later Edward VII) was the senior flag officer for nineteen years until he became King.

had increased the prosperity of Cowes significantly. Several large houses were built on both sides of the Medina and Queen Victoria's decision to build at Osborne in 1845 ensured continued growth and prestige for Cowes into the nineteenth century.

The keen interest of the Prince of Wales in yachting and the arrival of the Royal Yacht Club (later Squadron) in 1854 further enhanced Cowes' reputation and attraction. Another of Cowes' claims to fame has been as a home to shipbuilders, primarily J. Samuel White and Saunders-Roe, which made high-speed ships, seaplanes and flying boats. Saunders-Roe built Sir Malcolm Campbell's

PLACES TO VISIT

Cowes

Cowes Maritime Museum
Cowes Library, Beckford Rd
Displays covering the Island's maritime history in models, paintings and photographs. Open Mon, Tues and Fri, 10.00am–12.30pm & 1.30–5.00pm; closed Wed and Thurs. Tel 01983 823433

Sir Max Aitken Museum
The Prospect, 83 High Street, Cowes, IOW, PO31 7AJ
The Museum is in the old Ratsey and Lapthorn sailmakers' loft and displays Sir Max Aitken's collection of nautical instruments, paintings and other maritime artefacts. Admission charge. Open May-Sept, Tues-Sat 10am-4pm. Tel 01983 293800
www.sirmaxaitkenmuseum.org

▲ Sir Max Aitken Museum at Cowes.

The Centre of the Island

▶ The lion on Egypt Esplanade at West Cowes.

▼ Cowes Floating Bridge crosses the river Medina.

▼ Egypt Point lighthouse marks the northernmost point of the Island.

Bluebird and developed Sir Christopher Cockerell's hovercraft.

Today, the town lives very much on the tourist and yachting trades, with the focus of much of the activity in West Cowes, especially during 'the season', where the bulk of shops and hotels are located. The most appealing parts of West Cowes are the open, often bracing, but spectacular seafront and Prince's Green.

The HQ of the Royal Yacht Squadron is fronted by 21 brass cannons from *Royal Adelaide*, the yacht of William IV. These are used to start and finish races. Sailing takes place all year round, but organised events run between May and September. June sees the Round the Island race when up to 1,000 boats compete.

During Cowes Week in August the traditional event is the annual Regatta of the Royal Yacht Squadron, but eight other clubs also hold races and regattas. Around 900 competing boats and 6,000 crew members take part. The Admiral's Cup series is held on alternate (odd) years and the

last race of the week is the Fastnet, which, after a long run out to the south of Ireland, ends in Plymouth.

There is a short walk along the old Esplanade in East Cowes to the

PLACES TO VISIT

Medina

St Mildred's Church

Whippingham PO32 6LW

Includes Victorian exhibition, tea room and souvenir shop. Car & coach park leading to the Orchard and Picnic Area. Usually open Apr to end-Oct, Mon to Thur, 10.00am–4.00pm. Church services on Sun at 11.15am. www.iow.uk.com/whippingham-church

Butterfly World and Fountain World

Staplers Rd, Wootton PO33 4RW

Landscaped, sub-tropical indoor garden, butterflies, Italian and Japanese gardens with water features and fish. Small World has Jumping Jets water displays. Open Easter to Oct, daily, 10am–4.30pm. Admission charge. Tel 01983 883430 www.butterfly-world-iow.co.uk

Osborne House

East Cowes, PO32 6JX

See page 47

grounds of Norris Castle, which was built as a mock-Norman residence-cum-folly cum-farm for Lord Henry Seymour in 1799. In West Cowes, Prince's Esplanade offers a stroll of a mile and a half (2.4km) to Gurnard. Gurnard is a busy, popular seaside resort with a good beach. It adjoins Northwood Park and House whose twenty-six-acre gardens offer a variety of pleasant walks and sporting amusements.

The fifteen-acre site of the Isle of Wight Military Museum, which specialises in tanks and military vehicles, is close by at the former Northwood Camp. Tel 01983 527411, www.isleofwight militaryhistorymuseum.co.uk.

Around the Medina

Whippingham lies above the river Medina and, in medieval times, embraced a large area which included Wootton. Despite its early Jutish or Saxon origins, it has no discernible village centre and is very spread out. A footpath leads to

Sailing legend

Uffa Fox, born in East Cowes in 1898, was a near legendary yachtsman, who in 1928 managed 52 wins out of 57 starts (second in two races and third in three) in Avenger, a 14ft (4m) boat he designed himself. He also designed other racing yachts, including the famous Flying Fifteens and invented the air-deployed lifeboats, which saw service in World War II. Equally famous for his buccaneering lifestyle, he was the doyen of the Isle of Wight yachting scene and died in 1972.

PLACES TO VISIT

Porchfield

Coleman's Farm
Porchfield PO30 4LX

7 · 12 · 60 · 60

A multi-activity and play area, especially good for a rainy day. Hands-on experience with pet animals raised on the farm. Cafe and gift shop. Daily Mar-Nov, 10am-5pm. Tel 01983 522831. www.colemansfarmpark.co.uk

Centre Wight

the river from where there is a nice walk, suitable for birdwatchers, upstream to Newport.

St Mildred's Church is by origin medieval, but was completely rebuilt by John Nash in 1804. As the nearest church to the Osborne estate, this was selected as the church where the Royal Family

◀ Cowes centre.
▼ The Royal Yacht Squadron at Cowes.

Osborne House

© English Heritage Photo Library

Osborne House is a fascinating and revealing insight into the Victorian era and Royal family life, impressive both overall and in detail and attracting a great many visitors throughout the year. Osborne was built for Queen Victoria as a country retreat and family residence in 1845-8, 'a place of one's own, quiet and retired', away from the pressure of state ceremonial. It was her favourite residence after the death of Prince Albert in 1861 and where she herself died in 1901.

The present building was designed by Prince Albert, with the technical assistance of a leading London builder and entrepreneur, Thomas Cubitt. Osborne reflects the Prince's admiration for Italian art and architecture and the design is based on an Italian villa, with tall towers (campaniles) and a balcony

(loggia). The flag tower is 107ft (33m) high and the clock tower 90ft (27m).

After Queen Victoria's death, nobody in the Royal family was keen to live at Osborne, removed as it was from mainland society. Edward VII, who preferred Sandringham, gave Osborne to the nation as a memorial to his mother. The house first opened to the public in 1904 and its contents have remained substantially the same ever since. The State and private apartments used by Queen Victoria in the west and north wings are open to the public, as are the gardens. The Royal Nursery suite was opened in 1989.

Immediately on arrival through the Prince of Wales' Gate, it is interesting to note that the site of the former Royal Naval College (1903-21), which was a preparatory establishment for Dartmouth, is now the main car park. It is recommended that a tour starts with the Royal apartments inside the house and continues outside afterwards.

This may need to be adjusted depending on the weather or when the house is particularly busy. Within the house itself, the tour takes in a succession of public and private rooms, lavishly furnished and decorated, which contain countless personal memorabilia and gifts from all over the world. The breathtaking Durbar Room, the expression of Victoria's status as Empress of India and constructed in 1893 to a design by an Indian architect, contains many reminders and artefacts from the sub-continent.

Outside, on exiting from the Durbar wing, the upper terrace provides panoramic views and a pleasant stroll around the Royal Pavilion and Solent frontage of the house. It also looks down on the lower terrace, with its Andromeda fountain and pergola, but this part of the garden is not open to the public. The restored walled garden opened in July 2000 and the design incorporates the initials V & A throughout. There are two original glasshouses with a wonderful array of colourful plants.

From the house, a path leads for half a mile (800m) to the Swiss Cottage and museum, which can also be reached by minibus (free with entry ticket). The Swiss Cottage is a very up-market Wendy House, in the style of a Swiss chalet, built in 1854. It was originally thought that it had been prefabricated abroad and put together at Osborne but restoration work in 1990 revealed that the estate carpenters actually built the structure.

Prince Albert intended the Swiss Cottage to be an educational device to teach his children the rudiments of housekeeping and cookery. A suite of functional rooms, including a pantry, kitchen, dining and sitting rooms, together with appropriate furnishings and utensils, helped the royal siblings get into the spirit of things. It was also a place where the children could house their growing collection of gifts, mementoes and natural history exhibits. These curious and personal items are now housed in a purpose built (1862) museum nearby.

Other items are worthy of notice in the gardens. Firstly, there is the ultimate boys' play area. The Victoria Fort, completed in 1856, after the Crimean war, is in miniature just like the Palmerstonian forts, which guard Portsmouth. The royal princes assisted with its construction and Prince Arthur helped add the Albert Barracks in 1860. Also, alongside the deckhouse of the Royal Yacht Alberta (1864) is Queen Victoria's bathing machine, with its changing room and WC.

There is an excellent illustrated souvenir guide produced by English Heritage. Visit arrangements in the house are seasonally adjusted: in winter visitors are taken on pre-booked guided tours by the custodians; in the busier summer months free flow access around the tour route applies. Facilities at Osborne include a reception, shop, restaurant, cafeteria and toilets.

> Open 10am–5pm daily from 1 April to 30 Sept and 10am-4pm from 1–31 Oct.
> Phone for winter opening times, pre-booked tour details & entry prices.
> English Heritage members enter free.
> Postcode: PO32 6JX
> Telephone (01983) 200022
> www.english-heritage.org.uk

© English Heritage Photo Library

The Centre of the Island

► Wootton Creek, a tidal estuary that flows into the Solent.

PLACES TO VISIT

East Cowes

Classic Boat Museum
Albert Road, East Cowes
PO32 6AA. Tel 01983 290006

The Classic Boat Gallery
Columbine Road, East Cowes
PO32 6EZ. Tel 01983 244101
www.classicboatmuseum.org
Open Mar-Oct, Tues-Sat, 10am-
4pm, restricted winter opening

could worship. Nash's building was demolished and the present extraordinary amalgam of Victorian Gothic, mock medieval and personal whim was put up in 1854 and 1861. Some of the features are remarkable, notably a squat tower

Isle of Wight Lavender

At Staplehurst Grange, just east of Newport. Well worth a visit, this charming farm site has over 230 cultivars and lavender oil is distilled on site to produce a wide variety of oils, candles, creams and a full range of toiletries and gifts. Open all year, the Old Dairy Tearoom offers the famous lavender ice-cream and delicious cakes. Open Mon to Sat 10am–4.30pm and Sun 10am–3.30pm, closed Wed Oct to end-Mar. Long Lane, PO30 2NQ, telephone 01983 825272, or see www.lavender.co.uk.

with five pinnacles and the royal tombs and memorials, including one to Prince Albert, inside. Indeed, the church has so many Victorian associations and memorabilia that it struggles to maintain its sanctity amid the press of visitors.

In the churchyard is an iron cross, which marks the grave of Prince Louis of Battenberg, 1st Marquis of Milford Haven, and his wife, Princess Victoria of Hesse, granddaughter of Queen Victoria. They were the parents of Earl Mountbatten of Burma and grandparents of Prince Philip, the Duke of Edinburgh. By the north wall is the grave of Uffa Fox, famous yachtsman and boat designer.

Opposite the church are some Almshouses, which were built on the orders of Queen Victoria in 1880 for retired Royal servants. Similarly, Coburg Cottage in Mount Road was built in 1853 and designed by Prince Albert in the style of a Bavarian hunting lodge.

Also in Whippingham is Barton Manor. This medieval manor and Jacobean farm was bought by

Queen Victoria at the same time as Osborne House and robustly rebuilt by Prince Albert in 1845, to the veiled despair of local and national antiquarians. Used as an overflow for houseguests and the home farm for the Osborne Estate, its additional cooking facilities were frequently needed. Barton Manor is currently in private ownership.

Further east near Fishbourne, Wootton sits on a tidal estuary and has an attractive, restored church (St Edmund's), with Norman reminders. It and Wootton Bridge are mainly residential, with a beach at Woodside, although modern development and holiday centres crowd the scene. At low tide, the more adventurous will be rewarded with an energetic scramble over the rocks westwards to King's Quay (1.5 miles/ 2.5km return trip).

Just to the south-east, Firestone Copse is a delightful forest and waterside walk run by the Forest Enterprise. Something to watch out for on the main road in Wootton is the Minghella ice cream factory, of particular interest to Italian ice cream lovers.

Further south, Parkhurst Forest is a 1,100-acre (446 hectare), surprisingly unspoilt, tract of land, owned and run by the Forest Enterprise, which has a series of nature and forest trails for visitors. It is the only substantial piece of woodland on the Island and home to a large number of red squirrels. On the edges, but scarcely noticed by the walker, are the maximum security prisons – Parkhurst and Albany – and the short-stay Camp Hill. Parkhurst was originally a military hospital built in 1799,

Ghosts

The Isle of Wight has a thriving ghost industry, based on centuries of tales and legends, some of them eminently plausible, and 'genuine' sightings. It all very much depends on what you believe. Over 200 sightings have been researched and catalogued by Gay Baldwin in her popular books about Ghosts of the Isle of Wight. Some of these lurid tales feature in Ghost Walks led by guides in period costume, which begin at 8pm most nights at various locations throughout the Island from Easter to Halloween. Details are available in brochures and via the website www.ghostisland.co.uk, or tel 01983 520695. Advance booking is recommended.

which opened as a prison and convict transportation depot in 1838 and was later extended. Albany was purpose built in 1963-6.

Newport

Newport is the capital and bustling administrative centre of the Island. Founded as a market town and port in the twelfth century, on the lowest fording point of the River Medina, it received its charter in 1180. It reached the height of its prosperity in the eighteenth- century, during the Napoleonic wars and still retains its commercial character

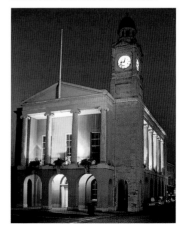

◀ Newport Guildhall lies at the junction of Quay Street and High Street.

Charles I and Carisbrooke

Some of the major events in the history of Carisbrooke Castle concern the stay and imprisonment on the Island of Charles I after his defeat in the First Civil War of 1642-5. During November 1647, when in negotiations with the Scots, Parliament and the Army about a settlement, Charles fled to the Isle of Wight, supposedly because of threats against his life by extremists in the New Model Army. He still had loyal supporters amongst the leading families of the Island, including the Oglanders and Worsleys and the Parliamentary Governor Colonel Robert Hammond was considered a moderate, with links to the Army Council.

On the King's arrival, Hammond, a 26-year old cousin of Oliver Cromwell, preserved the fiction that the King was a guest. In reality, Charles was closely watched while negotiations proceeded with the Scottish and English commissioners. However, he was allowed considerable freedom to move around the precincts of the castle, to go hunting and to visit local notables.

While stalling negotiations with the English commissioners, Charles had secretly concluded a deal with the Scots by which Parliament's erstwhile allies would invade England to coincide with a Royalist rising the following year. This would in effect mean a renewal of the Civil War. After rejecting all the English commissioners' proposals, Charles and his supporters decided that it was time for him to escape, but Hammond now dismissed the King's attendants and restricted his freedom further. The King walked under escort during the day and was locked in his chamber at night.

Royalist escape plots continued and eventually on 20 March 1648, Charles tried to escape through the first floor window of his lodging, but found that he had put

▶ Part of the Queen Victoria Memorial in St James Square in Newport.

today. Somehow Newport has just about kept its narrow streets, squares and a riverside. St James Square was the old market square until 1928 and is dominated by a memorial to Queen Victoria. The High Street contains some interesting buildings, including the Guildhall (1814-16) by John Nash and the Castle Inn (1684).

The shops have the familiar high street names, but many have hung on to their traditional character

on weight and the gap was not big enough. He was moved to another chamber and the ground beneath the window guarded by three soldiers. The gap in the window was enlarged by the removal of a bar with acid but another attempt on 28 May failed when the plot was betrayed.

During July and August 1648, the Second Civil War took place as had been planned at Carisbrooke the previous Christmas. The Army commanders, Fairfax and Cromwell, spent the summer and autumn defeating the Scots and suppressing the Royalist risings.

Charles now attempted to come to terms with the Presbyterian (non-Army) members of Parliament, in the so-called Treaty of Newport, in the face of an aggrieved and increasingly radicalised Army, which, after a second civil war, was calling for the trial of the King as a 'man of blood'. Then, in a decisive coup ordered by Fairfax, Hammond was arrested on 27 November and taken to the Army Council. On 30 November, the King himself was arrested and taken to London for a trial, which ended with his execution on 30 January 1649.

and building styles. Supermarkets and out of town developments have also proliferated in response to local and tourist demand. Newport Minster - St Thomas's - was originally built in 1173 in what is now St James Square, but the church was demolished down to its window sills and rebuilt in 1854 in the early Decorated style. Princess Elizabeth, the second daughter of Charles I who died in 1649, is buried in front of the altar.

The memorial in Carrara marble was erected in 1856, as 'a token of respect for her virtues, and of sympathy for her misfortunes' by Queen Victoria. Other highlights include a carved oak pulpit and stone font from the 1630s, and a memorial to Sir Edward Horsey, Captain of the Island 1565-82.

Carisbrooke

Anglo-Saxon sources and scanty archaeological evidence suggest

▲ Event at Carisbrooke Castle.

The Centre of the Island

Old Gallows

Close to Robin Hill is the Hare and Hounds, the second oldest pub on the Island, from which hangings are reputed to have taken place on Arreton Down. One of those executed and displayed on the gibbet on Downend Gallows Hill was Micah or Michael Morey, a woodcutter, in 1735. He killed his grandson with an axe and tried to conceal the murder by burning down their shared cottage on top of the body. His ghost has been seen to walk on a number of occasions, most recently 1974 in Burnt House Lane, around Robin Hill Country Park and near the Hare and Hounds. The skull in the pub, which has been claimed as his, is older and may have come from an archaeological site on the Downs. One of the rafters is said to be the crossbeam of an old gallows. The local superstition held that a piece of wood from a gallows helped ward off evil spirits.

PLACES TO VISIT

Newport

Carisbrooke Castle
Newport PO30 1XY
Large car park and
good places for a picnic. Open
Apr-Sept, 10am–5pm; Oct
10am–4pm. Nov-Mar, weekends
only. English Heritage members
free. Tel 01983 522107.

The Museum of Island History
Newport Guildhall, PO30 1TY
Dinosaurs to the present day
on touch screens and hands-on
exhibits. Open Tues and Thur,
10.30am–4pm. Tel 01983 823366.

Farmers' Market
St Thomas Square, Newport
Every Friday, 9am-2pm.

that Carisbrooke was the original capital of the Island in Jutish and Saxon times. Known as Wihtgarsburh, the town of Wihtgar, it probably gave its name at the time to the whole Island.

During the medieval period, Carisbrooke, with its castle and Benedictine priory, was acknowledged to be the main market and administrative centre until the coastal and fishing trade of Newport grew substantially in the sixteenth century. The main attractions today are the castle and the church, although the village itself merits a brief stroll.

Carisbrooke Castle is well worth a detour on account of its imposing situation, lively history and substantial, interesting remains. The site was probably occupied in the late Roman period by a rectangular fort with bastions. What is certain is that the Normans built a castle during the tenure of

► St James
Square, Newport.

◀ The village of Carisbrooke has a medieval parish church.

Newport

Roman Villa

Cypress Rd, Newport PO30 1HE

Discovered in 1926, three rooms have well-preserved mosaics; there is a collection of artefacts. Open Easter to Oct, Mon-Sat, 10am–4.30pm. Admission charge. Tel 01983 529720

The Quay Arts Centre

Sea Street, Newport Harbour PO30 5BD

Former 19th century warehouses transformed into an Arts Centre, with a cinema and theatre, as well as a café, gallery shop and bar. Varied programme of events. Open Mon to Sat. Tel 01983 822490. www.quayarts.org

Owl & Monkey Haven

7 – 12
60 – 60

Staplers Rd, Newport PO30 2NB

Landscaped rescue sanctuary for primates and birds of prey. Tel 01983 530885 www.owlandmonkeyhaven.co.uk

IOW Bus and Coach Museum

The Quay, Newport PO30 2EF

Transport Heritage and memorabilia. Variable opening times, so check website for details. Tel 01983 533352 www.iowbusmuseum.org.uk

PLACES TO VISIT

William fitzOsbern as lord of the Island. The castle still retains its classic motte-and-bailey shape, with a twelfth century shell keep and curtain wall, but has had extensive thirteenth century and later additions. The gatehouse is predominantly fourteenth-century and the internal buildings and artillery earthworks are from the Tudor period. Its attractive museum contains a collection of local archaeological and historic objects including personal relics of Charles I, transferred from Windsor Castle, and numerous paintings of local scenes and personalities.

Children are very likely to enjoy seeing the Well House, in which

▼ Minster of St Thomas, Newport.

Arreton Barns and Old Village

A popular commercially-oriented craft and curio village including the Dairyman's Daughter Pub and Tearoom, as well as leather, lace, lavender and glassware studios. Farmer Jack's farm shop specialises in fresh Isle of Wight produce. Also on site is the Shipwreck Centre, which contains a treasure trove of artefacts recovered from local waters, as well as ship models, and lifeboat and diving exhibits.

▲ St George's Church, Arreton, part of which dates from the 12th century.

▶ The Shipwreck Centre, Arreton.

a trained donkey draws water on a tread-wheel from a well 161ft (49m) deep and sunk in 1130. The water depth varies between 15-70ft (5-21m) and every time the bucket is raised the donkey will have walked the equivalent of 422yd (386m).

St Mary's Church, of early Saxon foundation, was started in its present form by William fitzOsbern in 1070, and restored in 1907. In 1156 the site was given to the abbey of Lyre in Normandy and the French Benedictines built a priory which incorporated the church. This priory thrived until dissolved by Henry V in 1414. It fell into ruin, but the church continued to serve the parish and its impressive tower was built in 1470. Look out for some notable memorials and graffiti from about 1440 outside the north wall of the church.

Further South

Gatcombe is a remote, scattered hamlet, with a manor house, thatched cottages and an abandoned water mill, set amid lovely scenery. Its largely medieval church, St Olave's, has the oldest stained glass on the Island and an east window by Morris, Rossetti, Ford Maddox Brown and Burne-

PLACES TO VISIT

Arreton

Arreton Barns and Old Village

Main Road, Arreton, PO30 3AA

Craft and curio village, including the Dairyman's Daughter Pub and Tearoom, gift shop, microbrewery, leather crafts, lace, lavender, glassware. Farmer Jack's farm shop. www.arretonbarns.co.uk

Shipwreck Centre

Arreton Barns Craft Village, Main Road, Arreton PO30 3AA

Open Easter to end Oct 10.30am-4.30pm. Tel 01983 533079. www.iowight.com/shipwrecks

7 12 30 45

Robin Hill Country Park

Robin Hill, Downend, Newport, PO30 2NU

Set in countryside on the Arreton Downs with activities for all ages. Open Apr to Oct. Entry charge but unlimited free return within seven days, closed during parts of Sept for 'Bestival'. Check website for details. Tel 01983 527 352. www.robin-hill.com

7 12 90 120

Jones. An early fourteenth-century wooden effigy of a crusading knight is associated with the (fictional) disappearance, during a storm and eclipse in 1830, of an infatuated local girl called Lucy Lightfoot. The village itself allows easy access to tracks up onto the Downs.

Arreton is dominated by a handsome Jacobean manor house, which offers five-star bed and breakfast (tel 01983 522604). The remarkably long village church, St George's, originating from Saxon and Norman times and containing many noteworthy details, was restored in 1886 and is well worth the effort of a visit. Guided tours and trail Work Books are available.

Rookley and nearby Chillerton are set in attractive and varied walking country. Rookley used to be the centre of the Island's gravel quarrying and brick-making industry. The modern Chequers Inn, through Rookley Green on the road to Niton, used to be a billet for Excise officers and is a free house. It has a large car park that can be used by walkers and, with food, amusements and an outdoor play area, is ideal for families.

The eighty-eight-acre (thirty-six-hectare) Robin Hill Country Adventure Park is owned by the proprietors of Blackgang Chine and combines downland views, nature trails and picnic areas with over twenty theme park attractions such as the Time Machine, a 440 yd (400m) toboggan run, and a tree top adventure course. 'Colossus – the ultimate thrill'- is a swing boat ride. There are also Roman villa excavations, adventure and fun play areas and woodland walks.

▲ Arreton Old Village.

PLACES TO VISIT

Godshill

Godshill Model Village

Godshill PO38 3HH

Impressive 1:10 scale stone model village, with dwarfed trees and 1:20 model railway. Open Mar, daily, 10am–3.30pm. Apr, May, Jun early-Jul and Sept, daily, 10am–5pm, dusk in late July and Aug, (Sat 5.30pm closing). Tel 01983 840270. www. modelvillagegodshill.co.uk

The Centre of the Island

▲ Godshill is probably the most photogenic village in the Island with its many thatched tea rooms and gifts shops.

It is mainly a summer attraction, but family events at weekends are organised in winter.

Blackwater is a good starting point for walks over St George's Down on the eastern side of the Medina. The highest point is 363ft (111m) and there are fine views down the Medina Valley to the Solent and the mainland beyond. Carisbrooke can be seen clearly and the view stretches all the way round to St Catherine's and Shanklin Downs.

Godshill

Godshill is probably the best known and most photogenic village in the Island. It is uncompromisingly a tourist trap with its daily invasion of coach parties and numerous tea gardens and souvenir shops. For all that, it is a charming, thatched roofed village and is still well worth a visit, even out of season.

It has a narrow, winding main street with tree-lined lanes and a church set delightfully on a hill, hence Godshill. Legend has it that the villagers tried three times to build the church elsewhere, but every time found the stones removed to the current site. All Saints is in the top ten of UK churches and attracts over 100,000 visitors a year. Yet another early medieval church belonging to the abbey of Lyre, it is notable for its unusual funerary monuments and a unique fifteenth century Lily Cross wall painting.

Further down, amid a host of tearooms and restaurants, the Old Smithy has a range of attractive, fashionable shops (open all year) and gardens; its light meals and home-made cakes are excellent. Its garden attraction, shaped like the Isle of Wight, incorporates models, grottoes, aviaries and the Godshill Witch. The Cider Barn sells very powerful cider, alongside an impressive range of preserves, oils, jams, wines and mustards.

West Wight

Yarmouth and the North Coast •
Freshwater Peninsula • Walking Routes •
Julia Margaret Cameron • Back of the
Wight • Compton to Niton • Tennyson •
HMS Pomone • Warhorse • Inland •
Wrecks and lifeboats

West Wight

Away from the bustle and built-up areas of the eastern coast, the western part of the Island, from St Catherine's Point to Alum Bay (known as the Back of Wight), is mostly a mixture of dramatic downland and precipitous sea-cliffs. The lower-lying land along the northern coast through Yarmouth and Newtown offers a gentler, varied, but equally impressive experience.

The downland hills and the rugged coast are full of unexpected delights and contrasts and the area has provided inspiration and relaxation for a host of literary figures. It is ideal for walks or a leisurely drive, with attractive, rolling countryside, peaceful villages and extensive views over land and sea.

The southern coast can be explored by bus, car and cycle along the Military Road (A3055) or on foot by the coastal path. This skirts the chines, as the steep, valley-like cracks leading to the sea are known, eventually ending up at the spectacular chalk cliffs of Freshwater Bay, Alum Bay and the Needles. The coast gives fine views of the sea along its entire length. The more energetic and adventurous visitors can walk along the base of the crumbling cliffs near the water's edge.

Alternatively, a stroll or drive around the villages and Downs inland is just as rewarding, particularly as many of the Island's leisure trails intersect on the Downs. Car parks and short, circular walking routes along the coast and inland are plentiful.

Yarmouth and the North Coast

Yarmouth is at least as old as the Domesday Book. It was given

▼ The Wightlink ferry Wight Light approaching Yarmouth.

◀ The bustling harbour at Yarmouth.

a charter in 1135 and was a medieval planned town, with its size restricted by its location on solid rock surrounded by the sea and the low-lying marshes of the estuary. As the nearest town of the Isle of Wight to the mainland, it used to export agricultural produce and livestock, while importing coal and manufactured goods. It, and the roadstead, was protected by a small, distinctive castle built by Henry VIII, which was further strengthened in Elizabethan and Stuart times. It is well preserved and has an informative exhibition.

Yarmouth is the entry harbour for the ferries from Lymington and is a pleasant, old-fashioned port, which retains its distance. It tends to attract those 'yachties' who reject the hype of Cowes and the estuary is full of moorings and leisure craft, especially in summer.

PLACES TO VISIT

Yarmouth All

Island Planetarium
Ft Victoria, Yarmouth PO41 0RR
Call for opening times; 20 per cent discount for booking in advance. Tel 01983 761555. www.islandastronomy.co.uk

7 — 12 / 90 — 120

Marine Aquarium
Ft Victoria, Yarmouth PO41 0RR
Open Easter to Oct, 10am-5pm. Tel 01983 760283. www.fortvictoria.co.uk

7 — 12 / 90 — 120

Model Railway
Ft Victoria, Yarmouth PO41 0RR
Open every day 10.15am-4.30pm, Apr-Oct; Thurs-Mon mid-Nov-March. Tel 01983 761553/754421. www.fortvictoriamodelrailway.co.uk

7 — 12 / 90 — 120

Underwater Archaeology Centre
Ft Victoria, Yarmouth PO41 0RR
Open Easter to Oct, 10am-5pm Tel 01983 761214, www. underwaterarchaeologycentre.co.uk

7 — 12 / 90 — 120

Yarmouth Castle
English Heritage, PO41 0PB
Open April-Sept every day except Fri and Sat; open Oct-Mar Sat and Sun only. Tel 01983 760678.

West Wight

▼ Golfing at Freshwater.

► Yarmouth Town Quay with a variety of small boats and yachts, and the ferry terminal.

Its shops, restaurants and pubs are inevitably geared towards the tourist and waterborne communities. That said, there is enough variety, quality and originality in the shops to interest and tempt browsers, typically in Anne Toms' art gallery and the second-hand Book Room

in Jireh Place. Self-catering and waterborne visitors, in particular, will be attracted by Angela's Delicatessen. Harwood's Chandlers and Ironmongers will command attention, even from landlubbers.

In Norman times, the estuary at Newtown was much larger than it is today and was probably the best natural harbour on the Island. A thriving port and market town, Newtown (formerly Francheville) was the oldest borough (1256) on the Island (and until 1832 a 'rotten' one as well), but never recovered after a French raid of 1377 and the silting of the estuary. Only a cluster of farm buildings remains on the original site. The eighteenth-century Town Hall is a gem almost in the middle of nowhere; it has an interesting collection of borough documents and a replica of the town mace on view. Generally open Tues, Wed, Thur and Sun afternoons, April to October. Check with the custodian 01983 531785.

Further inland and off the main road, the village of Shalfleet (meaning 'shallow creek') had, up

PLACES TO VISIT

The Needles

Needles Pleasure Park
Alum Bay, PO39 0JD
A loud, seemingly out-of-place gaggle of amusements, including rides, an adventure playground and gift shops and Alum Bay Glass. Some rides and attractions have individual charges. All day parking charge in summer. Open Easter to Oct, 10am–5pm. Tel 0871 720 0022. www.theneedles.co.uk

Needles Old & New Battery
Needles Headland, PO39 0JH
The Old Battery is open daily Easter to Oct, 10.30am-5pm. Closes in high winds, so check on the day. The New Battery has free entry but is only open on Tue and Sat, Mar-Nov. No vehicular access to either Battery.
Tel 01983 754722.

until the seventeenth century, a quay which could take ships of up to 500 tons, carrying coal and other goods. With its inn, manor house, water mill and thatched cottages it is worth a stop for its church and the food at the pub (the New Inn) alone. The church is mainly late-thirteenth century, but with a Norman doorway and tower, originally designed as a tower of refuge, hence the 5ft (1.5m) thick walls and former lack of ground floor openings. Unfortunately, it had been built without foundations on 10ft (3m) of slipper clay and had to be underpinned in 1889 to prevent its collapse.

The Freshwater Peninsula

The Freshwater peninsula is all but cut off from the rest of the Island by the River Yar that flows northwards from its source near Freshwater

Bay to the Solent at Yarmouth. This is West Wight proper whose seaside, dramatic scenery and countryside, as well as a wide range of shops and entertainment, make it a quiet, unhurried resort area, which rarely appears to be overwhelmed by crowds, even in high summer. It is ideal for a long weekend away from it all and there is something for everyone to enjoy.

Arriving on the Peninsula from Yarmouth, the visitor will come immediately to Fort Victoria Country Park based around another Victorian fort that commands fine views over the western Solent, close to the water's edge. It has free parking on the former parade ground, but is particularly crowded on yacht and powerboat race days. Unless arriving on foot from Yarmouth (20 minutes) or by bus (only in summer), it is approached by a winding, narrow road, but

▲ Yarmouth lifeboat in her berthing pen.

▼ The Needles, a series of chalk stacks, are the most westerly feature of the Isle of Wight.

61

Walking Routes

→ **The broad Yar estuary** has an undemanding, scenic four-mile (6.4km) circular walk which would ease down a good lunch. It follows the western edge of the picturesque estuary, returning along the old railway line. Just as it turns back to the north, a visit can be paid to All Saints at Freshwater and, if required, the Red Lion.

→ **The Hamstead Trail** runs for seven miles (11.2km) from Yarmouth to Brook across the Downs to the south, starting at Hamstead Ledge. The return can be co-ordinated with bus times.

→ **To the east**, the entire coast-line of the Newtown estuary and four miles (6.4km) of the adjacent coast [300 acres (122 hectares)] have been absorbed by the National Trust. The beautiful low-lying marshes of the estuary with fourteen miles (23km) of creeks are largely unspoilt and sign-posted footpaths lead from Newtown to a Nature Reserve, one of the least frequented and peaceful parts of the Island. It is a particularly fruitful spot for birds (especially waders) and children and adults will enjoy exploring around the estuary on a dry day, possibly around the special two-mile (3.2km) nature trail.

→ Recommended walks from Brighstone. **Brighstone Forest**, a 2.5-mile (4km) trail, with car park on the Brighstone-Calbourne road. **Worsley Trail** runs 15 miles (24km) from Brighstone to Shanklin. **Tennyson Trail** runs from Carisbrooke to Alum Bay, but Brighstone is a good place to intercept the trail and head west, to pick up views and Tennyson reminders, either returning along the same route or along the coast. The round trip is about 12 miles (19km).

Freshwater

Afton Park Gardens
near Freshwater PO40 9XR
The seven-acre site has something for everyone: a summer garden, an apple walk, plant nursery, wildflower meadow, orchard and café. Open every day in season.
Tel 01983 755744.
www.aftonpark.co.uk

Dimbola Lodge Museum
Freshwater Bay PO40 9QE
Photo museum dedicated to life and works of Julia Margaret Cameron. Open Tues to Sun, all year. Admission charge. Tearoom and second-hand bookshop.
Tel 01983 756814.
www.dimbola.co.uk

there is ample parking. The attractions are housed in the arches of a 19th century brick battery.

The Marine Aquarium contains a small collection of local fish and invertebrates, including the more unusual poisonous weevers and odd-shaped pipefish, and a tropical reef section. As well as a café, there is a small planetarium and a marine archaeology collection of locally recovered finds. A separate, modern building houses a large computerised HO Model Railway,

► Newtown Creek and the area surrounding it is a National Nature reserve which is mostly owned by the National Trust.

which claims to be the largest and most modern layout in the United Kingdom. At least twenty-five trains are running at any one time and visitors can operate some of the functions. It is obviously a must for railway enthusiasts and children will find it fascinating.

The seashore and woodland can also be explored along a nature trail (with way marks) or the coastal path. The stretch between the Fort and Yarmouth along the sea wall will take about thirty minutes, there and back. Overall, Fort Victoria is a good family attraction, especially on a rainy day.

Just outside, on the approach road, is the appealing Boathouse Café and Tearooms. Hurst Castle, visible on a long spit of the mainland, which all but closes the western end of the Solent opposite, is one of a chain of so-called 'artillery' forts stretching from Cornwall to Kent. They were built by Henry VIII in the 1540s to protect the south coast against invasion by the French and Spanish.

Other forts on the mainland are those at Portland, Calshot and Southsea and, on the Isle of Wight, Yarmouth.

Freshwater itself is a large, ill-defined sprawl that has grown around a scattering of hamlets, resorts and village greens. The church of All Saints, dating from the seventh century and incorporating Norman, other medieval and inevitably Victorian features, is well worth a detour. It has a great many interesting items and is notable as having been Tennyson's parish church. There are numerous memorials to the Tennyson family and Emily, Tennyson's wife, is buried in the churchyard. The Victorian stained glass is striking, especially the double window by G. F. Watts portraying Sir Galahad, which hides an interesting feature for the sharp-witted.

Totland Bay has a small, secluded and less frequented sand and shingle beach, suitable for fishing and bathing. Wide views of the Solent and Hurst Castle on

▲ Alum Bay is within sight of the Needles, and is noted for its multi-coloured sandcliffs.

West Wight

▶ The Needles lighthouse was built by Trinity House in 1859 on the outermost of the chalk rocks near sea level. The helipad was added to the top of the lighthouse in 1987.

the mainland can be obtained from the wooded cliffs above (along a path called the Turf Walk) or from the loftier Headon Hill, just to the south. Colwell Bay, immediately opposite Hurst Castle, has a long sandy beach (at low tide), rock pools and refreshments, which make it popular with families, and it does get crowded in summer.

The Needles are three jagged chalk teeth marking the western extremity of the Island and are its best known landmark. A fourth 120ft (37m) steeple ('Lot's wife') collapsed in 1764 and the third rock is today the base for an automatic lighthouse, whose 1785-1859 predecessor used to stand on the mainland cliff above. Road services end nearby at Alum Bay and a half mile (0.8km) walk will be rewarded with one of the most distinctive views in Britain.

Boat trips to the Needles operate from Yarmouth, Alum Bay and Freshwater Bay. An exciting chairlift, or 181 steps, provides access to the beach at Alum and its twenty multicoloured sands for which the place is famous. Also on site, Alum Bay Glass (open Easter to October) levies a small charge to watch glass being blown.

A pleasant one mile (1.6km) walk (or Southern Vectis open-top bus every thirty minutes in summer and in good weather) will lead to Needles Old Battery (1862), a restored Victorian fort which has a sixty-six-yard (60m) tunnel, a café and spectacular sea views.

Tennyson

Alfred, Lord Tennyson, the son of a Lincolnshire rector, was born in 1809. He began writing poetry at the age of eight. In his early years, he wrote prolifically on classical myth and medieval legend, but was only financially secure in 1850, when he published 'In Memoriam' and was appointed Poet Laureate. He married Emily Selwood in the same year. In the 1850s, he produced arguably his most famous poems, 'The Charge of the Light Brigade', 'Maud' and 'Idylls of the King' about the Arthurian cycle. Dying in 1892 and buried in Westminster Abbey, he is considered the most representative and popular poet of the Victorian era.

An Iona cross of Cornish granite stands high on the Downs. It is a memorial to Alfred, Lord Tennyson, raised in 1897, on one of Tennyson's favourite spots, although he was a habitual strider over all the Downs. The fine views from the memorial on Tennyson Down are worth the climb from Freshwater Bay, from Alum Bay or up a path from a car park just past the Highdown Inn at Nodewell.

Farringford House nearby was Tennyson's home from 1856 until 1867, when persistent crowds of admirers forced him to live at Aldworth, near Haslemere in Surrey, 'a haven of refuge against the invading Philistine'. The striking exterior of Farringford can be seen along a tree-lined drive. The house is currently undergoing extensive restoration and conservation work but there are self-catering

Radio transmission

In 1897 Marconi set up a 131ft (40m) high radio transmitter at the Needles Hotel with a receiver at Poole 18.6 miles (30km) away, to prove that his equipment could transmit across water and from shore to ship. A stone monument recalls the event.

cottages in the grounds as well as the Farringford Garden Restaurant (www.farringford.co.uk).

The poem *Maud* mentions 'the house half-hid in the gleaming wood' and the royalties paid for the house. Subsequent works enabled Tennyson to buy the land between Farringford and the sea so that the view should not be spoiled.

Freshwater Bay has been formed by coastal erosion and the sand and shingle beach is only about 440yds (400m) wide.

▼ Freshwater Bay is a small cove on the south-west coast of the Island.

► The village of Brighstone.

▼ Jimi Hendrix at Dimbola Lodge.

On sunny days, it does become crowded and the air can be bracing. There is a nearby golf course at Afton Down for those who cannot lie on the beach all day. A curiosity, which may be viewed in passing, is St Agnes church. It was built of stone in 1908 with a thatched roof, about 33 yards (300m) inland. For a breathtaking, circular ramble, easy access is available up on to Tennyson Down (three miles/ 4.8km) and on to the Needles (five miles/8km). Other walks can take in the variety of prehistoric remains on the Downs.

Dimbola Lodge was the nineteenth century home of Julia Margaret Cameron (1815-79), a pioneering Victorian photographer and friend of Tennyson, who established a literary and artistic salon around her in Freshwater Bay. It was a 'house indeed to which everyone resorted for pleasure and in which no man, woman or child was ever known to be unwelcome'.

After being converted into holiday flats, the building was purchased in 1993 by the Julia Margaret Cameron Trust and now houses a permanent testament to Cameron's work, as well as exhibitions of eminent photographers and photographic techniques. The museum is open all year round and there is an admission charge for the exhibition.

The Lodge also has a second-hand bookshop, whose varied, high-quality stock is well worth a browse. For details see www.

cameronhousebooks.com

Nearby on the Newport Road, garden lovers will enjoy a visit to Afton Park Gardens. The seven acre site has something for everyone: a summer garden, an apple walk, plant nursery, wildflower meadow, orchard and café.

Back of Wight – Compton to Niton

This coast between the Needles and Compton, with its towering, crumbling chalk cliffs, has probably the most spectacular scenery on the Island, much of it owned by the National Trust. Along the shore are numerous arches, stacks and caves, which can best be examined from seaward. Compton Bay has a fine sandy beach, which is good for bathing and suitable for surfing.

Coastal erosion close to Brighstone has resulted in the progressive exposure of fossil and dinosaur bones. In 1992 the curator of the IOW Geology Museum at Sandown was searching

for fossil remains and found a large rib, which led to the discovery of a spectacular brachiosaurus skeleton. Although not complete, it is one of the most impressive finds of its kind in Europe.

The area between the Downs and the sea combines sandy ridges and clay levels. Formerly, settlements lay along a track at

▼ The views from the Tennyson Monument on Tennyson Down are spectacular.

West Wight

HMS Pomone

In October 1811 the 38-gun frigate HMS Pomone was returning from the Mediterranean when she struck a sunken rock just south west of the Needles point. The crew were saved as were the guns and principal stores, but not before some crew members had drunk themselves into a state of 'extreme intoxication'.

PLACES TO VISIT

Mottistone

Mottistone Manor Garden (NT)
Mottistone, PO30 4EA
Open Apr to Oct, 11am-5pm.
Closed Fri & Sat.
Tel 01983 741302.

Niton

St Catherine's Lighthouse
Nr Niton, PO38 2NF

Ten-minute walk down to the lighthouse. Normally open Tue-Fri 1-5pm, at Easter and Whitsun and from mid-June to end-Sept.

Blackgang Chine
Niton, PO38 2HN

Open Easter to Oct, daily, 10am–5pm (7pm during half-term and Jul/Aug high season).
Tel 01983 730330.
www.blackgangchine.com

Shalfleet

Shalfleet Manor Estuary Safaris
One hour boat trip around Newtown Estuary.
Tel 01983 531235.

the foot of the Downs leaving the coast remote and exposed. A ten-mile (16km) stretch of coastal road, the Military Road, was built in the 1860s to improve defence arrangements in the event of a French invasion and allow more rapid communications with West Wight, but this was not metalled until the 1930s.

Coastal erosion has brought the road steadily closer to the sea with the movement measured by tiltmeters. This south-west coast has been eroded at a rate of 11.5ft (3.5m) a year, although some areas have seen losses of 98-295ft (30-90m) after heavy rainfall. Numerous paths allow access to the sea-cliffs, and lanes lead inland to the Downs and villages.

The Military Road leads eastwards to Chale. The church, St Andrew's, is exposed to the same weather, which has, together with the nearby Atherfield Ledge in

Chale Bay, filled so much of the churchyard. The memorials and graves of seafarers who perished on the treacherous coast nearby can be seen clustered around a twelfth-century church, painted by William Turner in his early

► Compton Bay is popular with wave and kite surfers.

▲ St Catherine's lighthouse, dating from 1838, is situated at Niton Undercliff, five miles from Ventnor and is at the southernmost tip of the Island.

years. Well frequented and used for storage when Chale was the smuggling capital of the Island, it has had progressive updates throughout the medieval period and in the nineteenth century.

The coast at this point is dominated by Blackgang Chine, plausibly named after a smuggling band active in the eighteenth century, but more likely deriving from the black clay cliffs and the word gange, meaning a pathway. The chine is a shorter than the forbidding and deep 4,592ft, (400m) long ravine it once was at the start of the nineteenth century.

Starting in 1842, Alexander Dabell built a scenic garden in and above Blackgang Chine to attract the growing numbers of Victorian tourists. Further extensions of the gardens and a range of entertainments have been forced to adapt to cope with the advance of the sea and the effects of erosion in a process of what is known as managed retreat. Indeed, in 1994, a third of the park was displaced.

Progressively, from the 1970s, the site, still owned and run by the Dabell family, has developed a forty-acre cliff top site containing a multi-layered and multi-themed park which will delight children. Children can play on many features including The Crooked House, The Musical Pet Shop, Triassic Dinosaur Club, Smuggler's Cave, the Weather Wizard, Rumpus Mansion and the Fairy Castle, as well as a Water Force ride, with rubber boats rushing down 100m runs.

There are over forty acres of animated indoor shows, rides and themed activity areas. Parents will have to content themselves with gardens, The Disappearing Village and Blackgang Sawmill – World of Timber. The park attempts to provide a balance of educational adventure and fun, but to be fair the fun and commercialisation rather predominate. In busy months, especially at weekends, the place is packed out and full of opportunities to spend money.

Close by, commanding views from a nature trail of 2.5 miles (4km) above the 500ft cliffs are

West Wight

▲ St Catherine's Oratory, also known as the Pepper Pot.

well worth the effort. Access can be gained from the View Point car park. Far above and almost out of sight, on the second highest point on the Island, is St Catherine's Oratory. It was built in 1314 as penance by the local landowner for a wrongly appropriated cargo of French wine. Until the 1530s, a priest maintained the light and prayed for those lost at sea. From a car park on the coast road below, a brisk climb up a well-worn footpath will be rewarded with outstanding views (an hour up and down).

The Hoy Monument, commemorating a visit by Tsar Alexander I in 1823 and later adapted as a Crimea war memorial, is visible high inland. Provision for a picnic would add to the pleasure, as even during the height of the summer season, the climb, which is not excessive, deters casual visitors.

Niton is a good starting point for rambles, but is an otherwise unremarkable residential village. Its church, however, dating from Norman times, has tabletop tombs, used extensively in the past for smuggling and hiding fugitives, and the graves of the St Catherine's lighthouse staff killed during a German bombing raid in 1943.

The southernmost tip of the Island is St Catherine's Point, which is occupied by the twin-towered lighthouse, built in 1837-40 and known locally as the 'cow and calf' (the smaller tower housed a now discontinued fog signal). The light is automatic, but former keepers give a stimulating twenty-minute

'Warhorse'

Mottistone was the home of General Jack Seely, whose famous horse, Warrior, was a real-life 'Warhorse'. Warrior was born on the Isle of Wight in 1908 and survived the whole First World War, from the battle of Mons 1914 to the end of the conflict, and died in 1941.

tour of the Victorian lighthouse, which includes a climb to the top of the 89ft (27m) structure and a view of its formidable lamp. Children will enjoy the climb and the unfamiliar features; adults the unusual theme and the stunning sea view.

Inland

The broad expanse of rolling downland set back from a coast that is nearly always in view, is part of the east-west spine of the Island. It is highly popular with walkers and cyclists, but never seems crowded. It can be enjoyed along several long distance paths or on shorter circular routes. The villages are easily accessible by car.

The centre of Brighstone is one of the Island's most picturesque villages. It is a first-class place to start a ramble or walk: there is a nature trail in Brighstone Forest and many trails on the Downs can be accessed. Its church has an abundance of medieval and later features and a memorial to a Victoria Cross recipient in the churchyard. A glance at the memorial boards to the Brighstone lifeboat reveals that 433 lives were saved over fifty-five Victorian and Edwardian years.

In the former main street, in an attractive terrace of thatched cottages in North Street next to a National Trust shop, is a tiny but

Wrecks and lifeboats

St Catherine's and Chale Bay have the highest number of recorded wrecks on the Island – fourteen in one night in 1757. Between 1830 and 1900 more than 270 ships were wrecked along the coast, mostly sailing vessels unable to cope with the strong Atlantic south-westerlies and the peculiar properties of the tidal streams around the Island. One of the most notorious, the Clarendon in 1836 and its widely reported total loss of life (mostly women and children), led directly to the building of the St Catherine's Point lighthouse. From the 1860s, volunteer local men crewed the lifeboats (under sail and oars), established from Brighstone and Brook, which rescued the more fortunate. The records of their considerable achievements can be seen in local churches, most typically at Brighstone. Jack Seely, the 1st Lord Mottistone, served as crewman, coxswain and supporter for forty years.

Smuggling

The Island has long been associated with smuggling because of the remoteness of its southern coast and its general proximity to the mainland. The eighteenth century saw the heyday of smuggling in reaction to systematic enforcement of Excise Duty on a range of imported goods, notably tobacco and spirits. Enormous black economy profits were to be made and the chines allowed easy, hidden access to the beach while vessels offloading were able to conceal themselves under the cliffs. The problem was so great that in the eighteenth century eleven excise officers guarded the seventeen miles (27km) between Ventnor and Freshwater. By 1836 sixteen coastguard stations along the Wight's south coast, numerous revenue cutters and two wherries offshore had just about managed to control the situation. Punishment was draconian by today's standards – imprisonment, transportation or years of service in the Navy.

church and pub make it well worth a visit, particularly around lunch-time. St Peter's church is full of interesting features with an especially well-written guide available on site. Family memorials, a fifteenth-century wall painting and a blocked arch through which the village's defensive cannon was previously wheeled out are just a few of the many details. Three large manor houses – North Court, West Court and Wolverton Manor – whose former residents are well represented on memorials in the church and churchyard – are in or around the village.

Mottistone is grouped around a delightful manor house, which has successively been the home of the Cheke, Dillington and Seely families. After a landslip in 1706, it became a farmhouse until bought as part of the estate in 1861 by Charles Seely of Brook House. His grandson, General Jack Seely, later 1st Baron Mottistone, organised the removal of 1,400 tons of soil and rubble covering the buried east wing, before moving into

worthwhile museum, which has mementoes of village life. Towards the coast, Grange and Chilton Chines can be reached by paths from the coast road and bathing at high tide in the area is quiet and enjoyable away from the crowds.

Shorwell is a pretty, neat village that sympathetically mixes stone cottages with thatched roofs and modern buildings. Its

▶ Set in thirty-five acres of rural landscape, Calbourne Water Mill contains one of the oldest working water mills in the country, dating back to the Domesday Book.

Mottistone, and, by the time of his death in 1947, had restored the manor house. His son, John Seely, an architect of distinction, had assisted in the restoration and bequeathed the estate to the National Trust in 1963.

The church dates from the twelfth century, with heavy alterations in the fifteenth and nineteenth centuries. Despite this, it has retained its medieval character and is worth a stop to look at the memorials and tombs. The chancel roof is made from cedar planks from the wreck off Brighstone of the barque *Cedrene* in 1862. Near Mottistone, on the hill above, is the Longstone, the remains of a Neolithic long barrow, which can be reached after a climb along a path from the manor house.

Brook is a quiet, unassuming and widespread village which takes its name from the stream that flows through it. The medieval church on its mound, St Mary the Virgin, was rebuilt after a fire of 1862 and retains very few original features. It contains a service board recording the exploits of the *George and Annie*, *William Slaney Lewis* and *Susan Ashley*, the lifeboats that served at Brook until 1937.

South of the Military Road, at Brook Chine, is a secluded beach

▲ Mottistone Manor is a National Trust property featuring a twentieth century garden next to an Elizabethan manor house.

Calbourne

Calbourne Water Mill
Newport Rd, Calbourne PO30 4JN
A collection of historic farm implements, set in a rural location. It is a convenient and restful place to stop for coffee. Open Apr-Nov daily, 10am-5pm. Tel 01983 531227. www.calbournewatermill.co.uk

Chessell Pottery Barns
Brook Road (near Calbourne), Yarmouth PO41 0UE
Decorating studio, gift shop and café. Open all year. Tel 01983 531248. www.pottery-café.com

PLACES TO VISIT

73

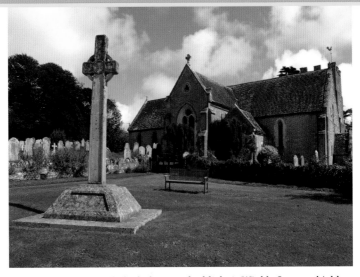

► Calbourne Church in the centre of the village.

▼ Brook Church. The medieval church burned to the ground in 1862, and its replacement is now the best preserved Victorian church on the Island.

near Hanover Point off which the fossilised stumps of a former pine forest, known as the 'pine raft', can be seen, covered in seaweed. J. B. Priestley lived in Brook Hill House.

Just to the north at Shalcombe is Chessell Pottery-Café centred in a large converted barn. For many years, the distinctive Chessell pottery was produced here, and you can now decorate your own pottery in a working studio.

The ancient manor of Calbourne is a cluster of thatched cottages, set amid fields and woods. The highlight is Winkle Street, a highly photogenic row of stone and thatched cottages opposite the river Caul. In the vicinity are two large houses: Westover, a large eighteenth century building, and Swainston Manor, now a hotel and restaurant, dating from Norman times and once owned by the bishops of Winchester. Swainston, an important estate held by many illustrious medieval families and the Crown, was substantially rebuilt in 1750, but retained many original features, notably the twelfth century hall and bishop's chapel. It was completely gutted by a German incendiary bomb in 1941, but has been carefully restored.

Despite its Saxon origins, Calbourne church today dates from the thirteenth century, when the estate belonged to the Bishops of Winchester, and has memorials to the present day. To the west of the village is the seventeenth century working Calbourne Water Mill with a collection of historic farm implements, set in a rural location.

Out and about

Motoring • Beaches • Public
Transport • Cycling • Walking • Manor
Houses • Themed Day Itineraries
• Churches • Bookshops • Literary
Associations • Gardens

Out and about

The Isle of Wight is a very flexible tourist facility and an ideal location for those based on the South Coast to enjoy a day trip or short break. Equally, there is a wealth of things to do during a longer holiday on the Island. It is an opportunity just simply to relax by walking the wonderful footpaths or by sitting in a deckchair on the beach. Many families frequently return to the Island and enjoy all the facilities that it has to offer. Even if the weather is inclement, there are plenty of options to keep both adults and children amused.

If you are spending a short time on the Island, planning makes it more worthwhile. In almost every case, a good map of the Island is essential, either from the Ordnance Survey series or the A-Z Isle of Wight Visitors' map.

Motoring

It is easy to take a car to the Island, which has nearly 500 miles (805km) of reasonable roads and direction signs, although motorists may wish to look at the off-peak pricing arrangements available from the ferry operators for crossing the Solent. As a matter of fact, mile for mile, it is the most expensive crossing in the world.

Once on the Island, the motorist will find that away from the prime tourist spots and town centres, the Island is relatively free of congestion. Newport, Ryde, Sandown and Shanklin can at times be very busy, but, generally, the Island is well served with traffic schemes and car parks.

Access is along metalled roads to all but the most remote visitor sites and most attractions have adequate parking. Petrol is usually one or two pence a litre more expensive on the Island. The many narrow country roads on the Island will inhibit speed and the only dual carriageway is in Newport.

Out of season, most of the more popular attractions can be visited

▼ Sunset over Compton Bay (National Trust).

in a single day. One day will allow a pleasant, leisurely drive around the whole coast of the Island, with regular stops. In season more time will be required and the day motorist will probably wish to pursue highlights or themes.

Beaches

The Isle of Wight has a great many beaches, most of which are suitable for bathing. Care should be exercised with regard to the prevailing wind and sea conditions, as well as the state of the tide. In terms of cleanliness, facilities and amenities, the Island's beaches continue to be nominated for and to win awards for excellence.

Ryde Has three wide, sandy beaches: Ryde West Sands, Ryde East Sands and Puckpool. Safe, shallow bathing with adult and children's facilities adjacent to the beach. Good for sandcastle building and has a seawater tidepool, but watch out for that tide coming in.

Seaview A well known spot for sailors and it has three beaches: Springvale, Seagrove Bay and Priory Bay. Rock pools.

St Helen's Bay This is good for swimming and has rock pools and a sandy beach. Behind the Duver are sand dunes, which are the habitat for lots of wildlife.

Bembridge Another well known sailing centre which has a foreshore on three sides. Beach and rock pools tend to disappear at high tide so timing is vital.

Whitecliff Bay Steep cliff access, but along a picturesque path. The sandy beach is safe for swimming, and there is a café.

Sandown With its long sandy

beach and developed facilities, Sandown is the ideal family beach, for both sand and swimming. It can get crowded though.

Shanklin Three adjoining beaches, Hope, Esplanade and Appley, provide a good, sandy shoreline in the shelter of steep cliffs. Access to beach is by road, foot or from the upper town via the lift. Good swimming and sandcastle terrain.

Bonchurch A quiet sandy beach with rockpools at low tide.

Ventnor This sand/shingle beach shelves steeply and has strong waves, next to a small esplanade. Bathing is safe, with opportunities for boating and angling.

Compton Bay One of the most popular beaches on the Island, a mile (1.6km) long stretch of sand, good for swimming and walking. It can be windy and is consequently frequented by windsurfers and

▲ Culver Down and Yaverland Beach. This chalky headland at the north end of Sandown Bay, is owned and protected by the National Trust.

◀ On the beach.

surfers. At low tide, pools of water are left behind, making it popular with small children. Older children may enjoy looking for fossil and dinosaur bones.

Freshwater Bay An attractive, sheltered bay with limited sand and pebbles. The beach shelves deeply so swimmers should take care.

Alum Bay Famous for its multi-coloured sands and scenery, the beach is pebbly. Strong tidal currents mean caution should be exercised. Access is by chair lift or on foot from Needles Pleasure Park.

Totland Bay A pleasant family resort and popular beach with safe swimming, the bay is sheltered and the beach has sand and shingle.

Colwell Bay A busy family resort with a long beach. At low tide a good stretch of sand is revealed, ideal for paddling, swimming and building sandcastles.

Gurnard Bay Good for family bathing, with a gently shelving sand and shingle beach. Surfing and sailing are possible and there are limited facilities.

West Cowes The sand and shingle beach makes an interesting viewing point for the sailing in the Solent.

East Cowes A good vantage point for watching the yacht racing. A children's paddling pool and playground are next to the beach.

Lifeguard patrols are a feature of three Isle of Wight beaches: Ryde, Sandown, Shanklin and Ventnor during the summer months May–September, 10am-6pm. Sandown and Shanklin have been designated European Blue Flag Beaches.

Public Transport

Buses Southern Vectis is the only company that runs an extensive network of public bus services on the Isle of Wight. The company produces a timetable twice a year, which is available on their website www.islandbuses.info. A variety of Rover or Freedom tickets is available, valid for one, two, seven

Themed walking trails

The following walks are suitable all year, except in extreme conditions.

The Bembridge Trail
Runs from Newport to Bembridge windmill through the southern part of the chalk downs, with some woods and good all round views. 15 miles (24km).

The Hamstead Trail
From Yarmouth to Brook passes though Newtown, agricultural land and the Downs. 8 miles (13km).

The Tennyson Trail
Runs from Carisbrooke to Alum Bay, taking in downland, forest and views of the sea, and is probably the most exhilarating walk on the Island. 15 miles (24km).

The Nunwell Trail
Runs between Ryde and Lake Common across water meadows, downs and agricultural land. 10 miles (16km).

The Shepherd's Trail
From Whitcombe Cross, near Carisbrooke, to Atherfield along mainly high downland with extended views. 10 miles (16km).

The Stenbury Trail
Between Blackwater (Newport) and Ventnor, passing through downlands and shallow valleys. 10 miles (16km).

The Worsley Trail
Goes from Brighstone to Shanklin along the southern part of the Island, with some forest and high-level walking. 15 miles (24km).

or thirty days' unlimited Island travel. In addition, Southern Vectis operates three double-decker bus tours every day in the summer – the Island Coaster from Ryde to Alum Bay as well as open top Breezer bus tours around the Downs and the Needles. Various other coach companies offer excursions around the Island.

Trains The Island Line runs from Ryde Pierhead to Shanklin. It has intermediate stations at Ryde Esplanade, St John's, Smallbrook Junction, Brading, Sandown and Lake. There are normally two trains an hour, The trains synchronise with Ryde Pierhead Catamaran arrivals. www.islandlinetrains.co.uk

Cycling

There are over 200 miles of cycle routes on the Isle of Wight offering the cyclist a vast network of country roads, bridle paths and rugged terrain to enjoy. Together with a well-marked 'Round the Island' Road Route, old railway lines and cycleways allow easy access to traffic-free areas.

For off-road enthusiasts, the Isle of Wight Council has details of mountain biking routes, which range from gentle leisure rides to day-long rides for the hardened enthusiast. www.islandbreaks. co.uk/site/sports-and-outdoor-activities/cycling. The Island hosts an annual 'Cycle the Wight' ride for charity as well as an annual week long Cycling Festival, usually in Sept. www.sunseaandcycling.com

Walking

The Island has over 500 miles (805km) of paths in an area of only 127 useable square miles (38,000 hectares). The Coastal Path can be

▲ The Shanklin Steamer Service operated by Southern Vectis, a hop-on hop-off service.

▶ Cycling along the coast.

walked in four days at a reasonable pace and is a series of constantly changing and contrasting views. Nearly half is preserved 'Heritage Coast' and its best bits are administered by the National Trust.

Inland, there are walks over downland, through unspoilt country villages and through woods and fields, which include some well signposted and maintained longer distance trails.

There is an annual Isle of Wight walking festival (www.isleofwightwalkingfestival.co.uk) as well as the annual Walk the Wight charity event in aid of the Island's hospice (www.iwhospice.org/walk-the-wight.aspx), usually both in May. In October there is an autumn walking weekend. Eight themed

▼ Walking along the coastal path at Alum Bay.

Histree trails are available to download at www.histreetrail.com. Further walking information can be found at www.islandbreaks.co.uk/site/sports-and-outdoor-activities/walking.

Manor Houses

The Island's wealth of manor houses, principally Elizabethan and Jacobean, are dotted all over the Island, but mostly in the inland south and east. Many serve as hotels, private residences and farmhouses, but some have access for the public. All have been mentioned in the text of this book but the best book devoted to the subject is The Manor Houses of the Isle of Wight by C. W. R. Winter (published 1984, now out of print).

Churches

Churches on the Island represent good way points for those who wish to have a theme or purpose when they travel. Virtually every village has a historic church of some sort, generally dating from Norman times, although many are not particularly memorable from an architectural point of view.

Coastal Path ↗

Suggested Themed Day Itineraries

Animals
- Owl and Monkey Haven – Butterfly World.
- Seaview Wildlife Encounter – The Isle of Wight Zoo.
- Isle of Wight Donkey Sanctuary – Isle of Wight Owl and Falconry Centre at Appuldurcombe.

Wallaby at Seaview Wildlife Encounter.

Food and Drink
- Rosemary Vineyard – Adgestone Vineyard - lunch in Ryde, St Helen's or Seaview.
- Farmer Jack's farm shop – Godshill Organics – Godshill Cider Company – lunch at the Garlic Farm.
- Wightlink has produced a leaflet called the Wight Taste Trail driving through scenic countryside and visiting independent farmers and producers en route. www.wightlink.co.uk

Gardens
- Nunwell House – Shanklin Chine – Ventnor Botanic Gardens.
- Appuldurcombe - Ventnor Botanic Gardens - Mottistone Manor Gardens.

Heritage and History
- Yarmouth Castle, Newtown Old Town Hall, Newport Roman Villa.
- Carisbrooke Castle - Osborne House.
- St Catherine's Lighthouse - Brighstone Village Museum - Needles Old Battery.
- Brading Roman Villa - Bembridge Windmill - Nunwell House.

Railways
- Model Railway, Fort Victoria - Isle of Wight Steam Railway at Havenstreet.
- Isle of Wight Steam Railway and Island Line journeys.

Keeping the kids amused
- Robin Hill Country Park – Amazon World.
- Blackgang Chine Theme Park – Fossil Hunting (Island Gems).
- Amusement arcades at Sandown or Shanklin – IOW Zoo at Sandown – Dinosaur Isle
- Shanklin Chine and the Undercliff.
- Needles Pleasure Park – Alum Bay.
- Godshill Model Village – Carisbrooke Castle.
- IOW Steam Railway and Museum at Havenstreet – Ft Victoria Model Railway.

Mosaics at Brading Roman Villa.

Out & about

81

▲ The twelfth century St Peter's Church at Shorwell.

communities, which take good care of their churches. They are generally open during daylight hours or the key is available from a willing neighbour.

The visitor will decide from the text those churches, which he or she wants to see, and may want to visit according to theme, geographic area or historic period. Certainly, those of Norman foundation, which include the majority, naturally group together, while the Victorian taste can be indulged in the resort towns of the South-East, at Whippingham and in Ryde. The churches that should not be missed are those at: Arreton, Brading, Brighstone, Calbourne, Carisbrooke, Godshill, All Saints, Ryde, Shorwell, Whitwell and Whippingham.

What they do have are a great many oddities, unusual memorials and curious features which crop up as surprises in practically every case and each one seems to have a story to tell. Most have been built with local stone, either limestone or Upper Greensand freestone except for Caen stone and Purbeck marble.

It will be clear that many of the parishes, particularly in the south and west of the Island, have thriving and enthusiastic

Bookshops

There are several second-hand and antiquarian bookshops on the Island, which will appeal to the general browser and specialist collector. Ventnor Rare Books, The

► Bonchurch old church dates from 1070 AD and is one of two churches in the village.

Ryde Bookshop and Cameron House Books at Freshwater Bay and The Book Room in Yarmouth to name just a few. They have a regular turnover of books, the prices are competitive in almost every case and the stock will appeal to a wide variety of tastes.

Charity shops and other secondhand/ antique/bric-a-brac outlets also stock an indiscriminate selection of titles, which are worth a browse, particularly in Newport and Ryde. Book fairs take place periodically, details of which can be obtained from any of the bookshops.

Literary Associations

The Isle of Wight is a fertile ground for tracing resident and transient authors and poets, as well as their associations with the Island: Matthew Arnold, W. H. Auden, Jane Austen, Lewis Carroll, Charles Dickens, Henry Fielding, Celia Fiennes, Thomas Hardy, Christopher Isherwood, Henry James, Frances Kilvert, Edward Lear, Henry Longfellow, John Keats, Rudyard Kipling, Thomas Nashe, Alfred Noyes, J. B. Priestley, Alfred Lord Tennyson, Aubrey de Selincourt and Algernon Swinburne.

Gardens

The Isle of Wight is known as the 'Garden Isle' because of its rich variety of different natural habitats and environments caused by subtle climate variations, the sea air and the wide geological diversity. Thus, contrasting characteristics exist within a few miles of each other, such as the pseudo-tropical conditions of Ventnor and the

Undercliff, the rugged salt laden south-west coast and the open chalk downlands. This diversity is reflected in the range of gardens on the Island.

Appuldurcombe House gardens were laid out at the end of the eighteenth century by Capability Brown. Skilful planting, serpentine drives, 'eye-catchers' and viewpoints on top of the surrounding downs created an illusion of size. Much of this is no longer visible but work is being carried out by English Heritage to restore the immediate park surroundings to their early nineteenth-century grandeur. There are currently eleven acres (4.5 hectares) of grounds.

▲ Thomas The Tank Engine events are organised by the Isle of Wight Steam Railway.

Coast & Country Scenic Drives

About 30 miles
Newport - Carisbrooke Castle - Chillerton (Gatcombe Church) - Chale Green - Chale - Blackgang - Niton - St Lawrence - Ventnor - Godshill - Newport.

About 35 miles
Newport - West Cowes - Porchfield - Newtown - Shalfleet - Yarmouth - Wellow - Calbourne - Brighstone - Shorwell - Carisbrooke - Newport.

About 35 miles
Yarmouth - Colwell - Alum Bay and the Needles - Freshwater Bay - Military Road - Chale - Chale Green - Shorwell - Brighstone - Mottistone - Hulverstone - Yarmouth.

About 35 miles
Ryde - Seaview - St Helen's - Bembridge - Yaverland - Sandown - Brading - Ashey Down - Mersley Down - Havenstreet - Whippingham - East Cowes - Ryde.

The Big One (around the Island), 75 miles
Newport - Arreton Down - Mersley Down - Ashey Down - Yarbridge - Sandown - Shanklin - Bonchurch – Ventnor – St Lawrence - Niton - Blackgang - Chale - Military Road - Freshwater Bay - Alum Bay and the Needles - Yarmouth - Shalfleet - Newport.

Out and about

Mottistone Manor Garden is modern in comparison with the age of the adjacent fifteenth and sixteenth-century manor house. There are three parallel gardens, approached by a flight of steps from the entrance courtyard: the rose garden, fruit trees under-planted in summer with vegetables, and the main walk, which passes between a pair of long colourful herbaceous borders. Higher up, grassy terraces are planted with differing pairs of fruit trees – quinces, plums, gages, apples and sweet cherries.

Nunwell House has five acres (two hectares) of beautifully set formal and shrub gardens. A great avenue of lime trees leads up to the front of the eighteenth-century house. The gardens were replanted in the early 1960s and the current owners continue to refurbish them.

Osborne House Gardens Fifty acres (twenty hectares) are open to the public including the formal Italian garden and terraces to the rear of the house. Sweeping parkland leads down to Swiss Cottage with the charming cottage gardens. Lebanon cedars, magnolias, rhododendrons and azaleas line the pathways around the estate and there is a delightful walled kitchen garden. Specialised garden tours occur in the summer.

Ventnor Botanic Gardens feature a wide variety of species. A walk around the gardens takes in the Mediterranean Terrace, the Rock and Scree Bank, the Victorian Sub-Tropical Palm Garden, the Medicinal Garden, the New Zealand Garden, the Hydrangea Dell, the Japanese Garden and the Americas Collection. The refurbished Temperate House displays mostly southern hemisphere plants. Open daily from March to October. Restricted opening in winter months. Visitor centre, shop, café and plant sales. See www.botanic.co.uk or tel 01983 855397.

Other gardens are open around the island from Bembridge to Brighstone and Shorwell to Shalfleet. For more details and dates see www.ngs.org.uk.

Datafile

**How To Get There • Events
• Accommodation • Pubs •
Entertainment • Taxis • Restaurants
• Sports • Water Sports • Swimming
pools • Useful Information**

How To Get There

The island is linked to the mainland ports of Portsmouth, Lymington and Southampton (all in Hampshire) by car ferries and highspeed passenger services. The three major operators are Hovertravel (08434 878887, www.hovertravel.co.uk), Red Funnel (0844 844 9988, www.redfunnel.co.uk), and Wightlink (0871 3761000, www.wightlink.co.uk).

Car Ferry Services

Wightlink • Portsmouth to Fishbourne, 24-hour service, journey time 45 minutes, with departures every half an hour during most days and weekends, or hourly at other times; Lymington to Yarmouth, crossing time 35 minutes, with departures every hour.

Red Funnel • Southampton to East Cowes, crossing time 60 minutes, with departures every hour on the hour from Southampton.

Foot Passenger Services

Foot passengers can travel on any of the car ferries or use one of the following faster options which take foot passengers only:

Hovertravel • Portsmouth to Ryde. High speed passenger Hovercraft, journey time ten minutes. Connecting bus service with nominal charge between Portsmouth and Southsea railway station and the Hovercraft terminal at Clarence Pier, Southsea. The bus service meets all hovercraft arrivals and departs from the railway station on the hour and half hour depending upon the hovercraft timetable.

Wightlink • Portsmouth to Ryde. High-speed passenger catamaran, every 30 minutes, journey time 20 minutes.

Red Funnel • Southampton to West Cowes. High-speed Red Jet passenger ferry, sailings every 30 minutes at peak times, journey time 25 minutes.

Red Funnel car ferries pass off Cowes.

Events

Many local, national and international events take place on the Isle of Wight. It is best to check details in advance either on individual websites or www.islandbreaks.co.uk . Some of the main events are:

May • Isle of Wight Walking Festival: family fun walks to serious walking
• 'Walk the Wight' charity event

June • 'Old Gaffers' Festival, Yarmouth, www.yarmoutholdgaffersfestival.co.uk
• Isle of Wight Festival, www.isleofwightfestival.com
• Round the Island Yacht Race, roundtheisland.org.uk
• Isle of Wight County Show www.riwas.org.uk

July • Carnival Season

August • Carnival Season (continued)
• Cowes Week, www.cowesweek.co.uk
• The Chale Show, www.thechaleshow.co.uk

• Isle of Wight Steam Show, Havenstreet
• The Garlic Festival, www.garlic-festival.co.uk
• Powerboat Festival

September • Apple Day Festival, Afton, www.aftonpark.co.uk/appleday
• Bestival, Robin Hill Country Park, www.bestival.net
• Cycle the Wight, www.cyclethewight.org

October • Autumn Walking Festival

▲ P1 Power Boat Festival Cowes.

The 'Old Gaffers' Festival, Yarmouth.

Accommodation

The range of accommodation on the island is extensive and has, to a certain extent, improved considerably in recent years. There is something to suit all tastes and pockets: the most basic camping sites exist with exclusive adults-only holiday centres and contemporary self catering units , homely B&Bs with prestigious hotels. The two main ferry companies (Red Funnel and Wightlink) produce all-inclusive holiday packages covering the full range of accommodation on the Island and could be a good place to start.

Catered accommodation

Expensive

The George Hotel, Yarmouth (below)
www.thegeorge.co.uk
☎ 01983 760331

The Hambrough Hotel, Ventnor
www.robert-thompson.com
☎ 01983 856333

The Hermitage Hotel, Whitwell
www.hermitage-iow.co.uk
☎ 01983 730010

The Lakeside Park Hotel
www.lakesideparkhotel.com
☎ 01983 882266

The Priory Bay Hotel, St Helen's
www.priorybay.co.uk
☎ 01983 613146

The Royal Hotel, Ventnor
www.theroyalhoteliow.co.uk
☎ 01983 852186

The Seaview Hotel
www.seaviewhotel.co.uk
☎ 01983 612711

Middle range
Hillside Hotel Ventnor
  www.hillsideventnor.co.uk
  ☎ 01983 852271
Keats Green Hotel
  www.keatsgreenhotel.co.uk
  ☎ 01983 862742
Newnham Farm, Binstead
  www.newnhamfarm.co.uk
  ☎ 01983 882423
Premier Inn Newport
  www.premierinn.com
  ☎ 0871 527 8556
Rylstone Manor
  www.rylstone-manor.co.uk
  ☎ 01983 862806
St Veronica's, Bembridge
  www.stveronicasiow.co.uk
  ☎ 01983 872872
Travelodge, Newport
  www.travelodge.co.uk
  ☎ 0871 984 6348

Bed and Breakfast
Gotten Manor, Chale
  www.gottenmanor.co.uk
  ☎ 01983 551368
Lisle Combe
  www.lislecombe.co.uk
  ☎ 01983 852582
Mottistone Manor Farmhouse
  www.bolthols.co.uk
  ☎ 01983 740207
North Court, Shorwell
  www.northcourt.info
  ☎ 01983 740415
Redway Farm
  www. bedbreakfast.redwayfarm.co.uk
  ☎ 01983 865228
Strang Hall
  www.strang-hall.co.uk
  ☎ 01983 753169

Self Catering
Chilton Farm Cottages, Brighstone
  www.chiltonfarm.co.uk
  ☎ 01983 740338
Appuldurcombe Farm, Wroxall
  www.appuldurcombe.co.uk
  ☎ 01983 840188
Alternatively there are several rental
  agencies that can be contacted directly:
Isle of Wight Farm & Country Holidays
  www.wightfarmholidays.co.uk
Home from Home Holidays
  www.homefromhomeiow.co.uk
  ☎ 01983 854340
Wight Coast Holidays
  www.wightcoastholidays.co.uk
  ☎ 01983 873163

Holiday parks/centres

Holiday parks/centres/villages provide
a wide range of accommodation either in
mobile homes, bungalows, lodges, chalets
or apartments. This type of holiday is
ideal for those who want the maximum
facilities close to their accommodation.
Prices for accommodation vary but this
choice of holiday is ideal for larger families
and where saving money is essential.
The centres range from small family run
enterprises to large national companies.

Camping & Caravanning

There are plenty of camping and touring
sites for caravanners and campers. Set
in a variety of locations, both coastal and
countryside, some offer a good range of
facilities while others offer peace and quiet.

Youth Hostels

There are two hostels on the island: one
at Totland Bay and a summer hostel at
Brighstone. See www.yha.org.uk.
  ☎ 01983 752165.

Datafile

Pubs

▲ The Hare and Hounds pub at Arreton has an extensive menu.

The Island has a rich variety of hostelries, all different in character and atmosphere. The pubs selected are personal favourites of the authors.

Arreton • The Hare and Hounds: at the top of Arreton Downs, next to the Robin Hill Country Park, one of the oldest island pubs. Extensive menu with changing daily specials. Children welcome. 01983 523446

Chale • The Wight Mouse Inn – Extremely popular family pub serving an excellent range of food, caters particularly well for children. Superb views towards Needles and Tennyson Down. 01983 730431

Freshwater • The Red Lion – Next to All Saints church. A comfortable pub, good range of food both lunchtime and evening. Children under ten allowed only in the garden. 01983 754925

Godshill • The Taverners in the centre of the village offers a traditional menu using local produce. Kids menu for under 10s. Small garden with play area. Tel 01983 840707. www.thetavernersgodshill.co.uk

Hulverstone • The Sun Inn: close to Brook Chine on the Mottistone to Brook road. Great views from garden. 01983 741124. www.sun-hulverstone.com

Ningwood • The Horse and Groom: on the main road at Ningwood on the Yarmouth to Newport road. Great childrens' play area and menu. 01983 760672. www.horse-and-groom.com

Niton • The Buddle Inn: an extremely popular, hospitable pub, en route to and from St Catherine's Point Lighthouse. 01983 730243. www.buddleinn.co.uk

Shalfleet • New Inn: traditional village pub with small family area. Opposite the church. Excellent food served in the extensive restaurant. 01983 531314. www.thenew-inn.co.uk

Shanklin • The Village Inn – Old Village: extensive menu from salad platters to steaks. Children welcome. Garden. 01983 862514.

• The Crab Inn – Old Village: small children's play area. Serves food. No garden but small area to sit outside and watch the world go by. 01983 862363.

Shorwell • The Crown Inn – A typical village local with a large garden and bar area. Diverse menu. Popular with walkers, motorists and visitors to the nearby church. Families welcome, children's play area. 01983 740293.

Ventnor • The Spyglass Inn. Wonderful location overlooking the sea. Renowned for its local fish dishes, particularly crab sandwiches. Children welcome. 01983 855338. www.thespyglass.com

Whitwell • The White Horse Inn: supposedly the oldest pub on the Isle of Wight. With outdoor lawned area so good for families. 01983 730375. www.thewhitehorsewhitwell.co.uk

Entertainment

Night Clubs

Away from the hotels, the clubbing scene is centred on the larger holiday towns. Most operate a dress code. Smart casual is always safe. Southern Vectis runs a bus on Fridays and Saturdays for nightclubbers to a variety of destinations.

Newport • Temptation Nightclub, Lower St James Street, PO33 5HB
☎ 01983 559228
www.temptationnightclub.net

Sandown • Colonel Bogey's Nightclub, Culver Parade, PO36 8AT
☎ 01983 403658
www.bogeysnightclub.co.uk

Cinemas

Cineworld Multiplex Cinema
Coppins Bridge, Newport
☎ 0871 2002000
www.cineworld.co.uk/cinemas/39

Commodore Cinema, Star Street, Ryde
☎ 01983 564064
www.leoleisurecommodore.co.uk

▲ Newport Cinema Complex at Coppins Bridge.

Radio Stations

Isle of Wight Radio 102FM and 107FM
www.iwradio.co.uk

Theatres

Apollo Theatre, Pyle Street, Newport
☎ 01983 527267
www.apollo-theatre.org.uk

Medina Theatre, Mountbatten Centre, Fairlee Road, Newport
☎ 01983 527020
www.medinatheatre.co.uk

Ryde Theatre, Lind Street
☎ 01983 568099
www.rydetheatre.co.uk

Shanklin Theatre, Steephill Road
☎ 01983 868000
www.shanklintheatre.com

Supermarkets

Co-operative Stores in Cowes, Freshwater, Rookley, Sandown, Shanklin and Ryde
Morrisons, South Street, Newport
Sainsbury's, Foxes Road, Newport
Tescos, Brading Road, Ryde
Waitrose, Well Road, East Cowes

Taxis

Bembridge • Bembridge & Harbour Taxis 01983 874132; **Cowes** • Anywhere Taxi 01983 281711, Rounsevell Taxis 01983 280800; **Newport** • Amar Cabs 01983 522968, Solo Cars 01983 525010, 3Cs 01983 825029; **Ryde** • Amber Cabs 07977 846823, IOW Taxis 01983 617027, Lil's Taxis 01983 562130, Q Cars, 01983 810810, Ryde Taxis 01983 811111; **Shanklin** • A Cabs 01983 866772; **Ventnor** • B&B Taxis 01983 855181; **Yarmouth** • Yarmouth Taxi 01983 760024; **Portsmouth** • Aquacars 02392 666666.

Restaurants

The Island has a vast selection of places to eat from the expensive to the cheap and cheerful. Some restaurants and cafés are open all year, others seasonally, but wherever you find yourself on the island you are never far away from a cream tea or a good wholesome meal. Most of the larger hotels have excellent restaurants open to non-residents and some have been included in the recommendations.

Bonchurch • The Pond Cafe, Bonchurch: the terrace overlooks Bonchurch pond and serves imaginative dishes using local produce. Open for lunch and dinner. Medium price range. 01983 855666. www.robert-thompson.com

Freshwater Bay • Farringford Garden Restaurant: set in the grounds of the former home of Alfred, Lord Tennyson. Open daily for lunch and dinner, closed Mon & Sun evenings. 01983 752700. www.farringford.co.uk

Godshill • Old Smithy Coffee Shop: One of the best tearooms on the Island, open all year round. Delicious homemade cakes and lunchtime specials. 01983 840364. www. oldsmithy.com.

• Willow Tree Tea Gardens and Restaurant: Attractive gardens centred around a willow tree planted in 1914. Cream teas speciality, but a good spot for lunch. Seasonal opening. 01983 840633. www.willowtreegardens.co.uk.

St Helen's • Dan's Kitchen: overlooking the Green, this new bistro is open most evenings and for Sunday lunch. 01983 872303. www. danskitcheniow.co.uk.

Seaview • SeaView Hotel Restaurant: Close to the sea and using Island produce, this well-known establishment comprises two restaurants and a bar. Exotic seafood is a speciality. Booking recommended. Expensive but worth it. 01983 612711.

• The Priory Bay Hotel, Brasserie & Restaurant: Modern European cuisine in great location overlooking the Solent. Expensive. 01983 613146. www.priorybay.co.uk

Steephill • The Boathouse Restaurant, Steephill Cove: good for fresh lobster and crab. Open lunchtimes only, May to Sept. Booking recommended. 01983 852747.

Ventnor • The Hambrough: One of the most acclaimed Island restaurants which overlooks Ventnor Bay and uses local produce. The chef patron has a national reputation. Open for lunch and dinner. Medium-expensive price. 01983 856333. www.robert-thompson.com

• The Royal Hotel: A large elegant restaurant serving excellent food. Medium price range. 01983 852186, www.royalhoteliow.co.uk

Wootton • The Lakeside Park Brasserie: a stylish new restaurant with views across the lake (pictured below). Eat inside or al fresco. Medium-expensive. Open daily 12-9.30pm. 01983 882266. www.lakesideparkhotel.com

Yarmouth • George Hotel Brasserie: Next to the castle. Food is imaginative and decorative. View of garden and sea from dining room. Meals can be served outside. Medium-expensive. 01983 760331. www.thegeorge.co.uk.

Sports

Aerial sports • Flying training courses and half-hour trial lessons are available at the Isle of Wight Airport Specialist Flying School (Sandown) in Grumman aircraft or in a helicopter, 01983 402402. Hang-gliding and paragliding on the Downs. Butterfly Paragliding 01983 731611, and High Adventure 01983 741484 provide tuition. Vectis Gliding Club offer flights and lessons from Bembridge, 07870 165044.

Angling • There are opportunities for coarse fishing at Rookley Country Park and three commercial lakes at Nettlecombe Farm, Whitwell, 01983 730783. Sea fishing takes place from piers and beaches while boat trips offshore and to the banks and forts of the Solent are popular and easy to arrange. **Cachalot**: boats out of Bembridge for up to 12 people. 01983 872185 or cachalot-charters.co.uk. **Scotties Tackle** shops are at Newport 01983 522115 and Sandown 01983 404555; worth consulting on local conditions and facilities.

Fitness Centres • **Urban Metro Gym**, Smallbrook Stadium, near Ryde 01983 612000; **Urban Metro Gym**, Medina Court, Arctic Road, West Cowes, 01983 292925, www.urbanmetrogym.co.uk; **Fitness Factory**, 1a Portland Street, Newport, 01983 528149, www.fitnessfactoryiw.co.uk

Golf • Visitors are welcome at all Island golf courses, with varying time, membership and experience requirements. A telephone call will confirm details. Green fees are £15-25 per day, with the exception of Westridge, Ryde which is cheaper. **Golf courses** • **18-hole**: Freshwater Bay Golf Club 01983 752955, Shanklin & Sandown Golf Club 01983 403217.

12-hole: Ventnor Golf Club 01983 853326. **9-hole**: Cowes Golf Club 01983 292303, St George's Down Newport 01983 525076, Osborne Golf Club 01983 295421, Ryde Golf Club 01983 614809. **9-hole pay as you play** Westridge Golf Centre, Brading Road, Ryde 01983 613131, Floodlit Driving Range, golf shop, senior and junior tuition. **Putting and Crazy or Mini Golf** • Brown's Family Golf Course, Culver Parade, Sandown has two 12-hole pitch and putt courses, a 15-hole long shot putting range and an 18-hole bantam putting course, open Easter to September, 01983 402447. Other courses at Sandham Grounds, Sandown; Esplanade Gardens, Shanklin; Northwood Park, West Cowes; Appley Park, Ryde; and Puckpool Park, Seaview.

Ice skating • Planet Ice – Recreational skating and skates for hire, 01983 615155.

Leisure centres • The Medina Leisure Centre, Newport, 01983 523767. The Heights Health & Leisure Base Broadway, Sandown, 01983 405594.

Racquet Sports • **tennis** courts are available at: Newport (Seaclose Park – three courts and a skate park), East Cowes (the Esplanade), West Cowes (Northwood Park – six courts), Ryde (Puckpool Park), Sandown (Sandham Gardens – five courts), Ventnor (Ventnor Park); Medina Leisure Centre at Newport 01983 523767 has an indoor short tennis and **badminton** courts; **s**quash at The Heights Health and Leisure Base, Broadway, Sandown, 01983 405594.

Ten-pin bowling • Superbowl, Ryde Esplanade, modern ten-pin bowling alley with electronic scoring, 01983 617070.

Water Sports

Sailing • The Island offers unrivalled facilities for both power and sailing craft, with numerous marinas and yacht clubs. Two suggestions for those not bringing their own craft are: Yacht charter – Windward Sailing, 01983 612800 or www.windwardsailing.co.uk; Medina Valley Centre – RYA recognised sailing centre for all ages. Tel 01983 522195 or www.medinavalleycentre.org.uk

Wind/kite-surfing and surfing •
Wight Waters, Sandown – tuition for surfing, bodyboarding, sailing, windsurfing, kayaking and wakeboarding, as well as splash sessions, three-hour water sports sessions for families, 01983 404987 and www.wightwaters.com.

Earth, Wind and Water, Shanklin 01983 866269.

Surfing • Compton Bay is the pre-eminent place for surfing. The book to have is Sail and Surf the Isle of Wight by Stan Connolly and Staci Rivers.

Windsurfing • Learners will find the shallow and safe Seagrove Bay at Seaview and Silver Beach at Bembridge suitable places to avoid early embarrassment. The more experienced will want to chance their arm at Ryde, Yaverland, Gurnard and Compton and avoid the crowds on the more popular beaches. The really adventurous can be found out in the Solent and, occasionally, in the Coastguard Rescue Helicopter.

Other waterborne activities • Shalfleet Manor Estuary Safaris, Shalfleet, 01983 531235; Island Youth Water Activities, Cowes, 01983 293073; Bembridge Outboards Rib hire for qualified sailors, 01983 872817.

Swimming pools

The Heights Health and Leisure Base • Broadway, Sandown (main and learner pool, with a café and gymnasium). 01983 405594.

Medina Leisure Centre • Fairlee Road, Newport (25m pool, learner pool and slide). 01983 523767.

Ryde Waterside Pool • The Esplanade, Ryde (has a moveable roof and an outdoor paddling pool). 01983 563656.

West Wight Swimming Pool • Queens Road, Freshwater (also has a large sports hall, gym and multi-purpose room). 01983 752168.

IOW Sports Club • Seaview, 01983 613108

Ryde Swimming Pool and Boating Lake.

General Information

Car Hire – Self Drive
South Wight Rentals
Shanklin 01983 864263
1st Call
Sandown 01983 400055
Top Gear
Cowes 01983 299056

Cycle Hire
Wight Cycle Hire
Yarmouth 01983 761800
www.wightcyclehire.co.uk
1st Call
Sandown 01983 400055
Top Gear Cowes 01983 299056
www.isleofwighthire.co.uk

Farm Shops
Godshill Organics, Godshill
   Newport Road PO38 8LY, 01983 840723
Briddlesford Lodge Farm, Wootton
   Brindlesford Road PO33 4RY
   01983 884650
Farmer Jack's 01983 527530
   Arrreton Barns, Arreton PO30 3AA
Kings Manor Farm 01983 754401
   Copse Lane, Freshwater PO40 9TL

Farmers Markets
Every Friday – St Thomas's Square,
Newport 9am-2pm
Every Saturday – Town Square,
Ryde 8.30am-1pm

Useful Information

Tourist Information
The Isle of Wight no longer has Tourist
Information Centres but information is
available from Southern Vectis:
• Newport Bus Station Travel Office
• Ryde Esplanade Bus Station Travel Office
• Yarmouth Quayside Travel office
In the summer three mobile information
points are also operated by Southern Vectis
and parked at prime location bus stops in
Cowes, Sandown and Shanklin.

Websites
www.islandbreaks.co.uk
   Isle of Wight Tourism official website
www.isleofwight.com
   General information
www.iwight.com
   Isle of Wight council website
www.wightstay.co.uk Outline
   information about the Island

www.wightonline.co.uk
   Another general information site
www.isleofwighttouristguide.com
   More info about the island
www.english-heritage.org.uk
www.nationaltrust.org.uk

Maps
Ordnance Survey
OS Outdoor Leisure 29, Isle of Wight,
2.5 inches: 1 mile/4cm:1km.
Ordnance Survey Landranger 196,
Solent and the Isle of Wight, 1.25
inches:1 mile/2cm:1km.

Local Paper
Isle of Wight County Press
Published weekly, every Friday.
Up-to-date information on events can also
be found on the paper's website
www.iwcp.co.uk.

Datafile

Index